2004

Music in South India

Music in South India

The Karṇāṭak Concert Tradition and Beyond

EXPERIENCING MUSIC, EXPRESSING CULTURE

T. VISWANATHAN
MATTHEW HARP ALLEN

New York Oxford
Oxford University Press
2004

Oxford University Press

Oxford New York
Auckland Bangkok Buenos Aires Cape Town Chennai
Dar es Salaam Delhi Hong Kong Istanbul Karachi Kolkata
Kuala Lumpur Madrid Melbourne Mexico City Mumbai
Nairobi São Paulo Shanghai Taipei Tokyo Toronto

Published by Oxford University Press, Inc.
198 Madison Avenue, New York, New York 10016
http://www.oup-usa.org

Library of Congress Cataloging-in-Publication Data
Viswanathan, T.
Music in South India : experiencing music, expressing culture / by T. Viswanathan and Matthew Harp Allen.
p. cm.—(Global music series)
Includes bibliographical references and indexes.
ISBN 0-19-514590-9—ISBN 0-19-514591-7 (pbk.)
1. Music—India—History and criticism. 2. Carnatic music—History and criticism. I. Allen, Matthew Harp. II. Title. III. Series.

ML338.V57 2003
780'.954'8—dc21

2003053091

Printing number: 9 8 7 6 5 4 3 2 1

Printed in the United States of America
on acid-free paper

GLOBAL MUSIC SERIES

General Editors: Bonnie C. Wade and Patricia Shehan Campbell

Music in East Africa, Gregory Barz
Music in Central Java, Benjamin Brinner
Teaching Music Globally, Patricia Shehan Campbell
Carnival Music in Trinidad, Shannon Dudley
Music in Bali, Lisa Gold
Music in Ireland, Dorothea E. Hast and Stanley Scott
Music in the Middle East, Scott Marcus
Music in Brazil, John Patrick Murphy
Music in America, Adelaide Reyes
Music in Bulgaria, Timothy Rice
Music in North India, George Ruckert
Mariachi Music in America, Daniel Sheehy
Music in West Africa, Ruth M. Stone
Music in South India, T. Viswanathan and Matthew Harp Allen
Music in Japan, Bonnie C. Wade
Thinking Musically, Bonnie C. Wade
Music in China, J. Lawrence Witzleben

Photo courtesy of Wesleyan University.

Dedication

These prefatory pages are the only ones in the book that my co-author T. Viswanathan and I did not write together. Viswa passed away in September 2002, as we were approaching the completion of this project. His going leaves a huge hole that can not be filled for those who love him, but still, in the midst of our grief, a tremendous affirmation of life. The songs and skills he taught, the sound of his voice and flute, the jokes he told, the recipes he invented—they remain with us, part of his living legacy.

Like his flute-playing colleague Kṛṣṇa, by whom all the *gōpi* cowherd maidens felt loved, Viswa gave each of his students an amazing quality of attention. Our lessons and practice ushered us into the universe of his total involvement with music, which must be one of the highest manifestations of love. He honored us by judging our work with the same critical scrutiny that he levied upon himself. As with his namesake Śiva, whose third eye destroys impurity of all kinds, an appropriate glance from Viswa always incinerated pretensions and restored perspective. If I had not worked enough before a vocal lesson or simply could not master some material, he would flash his Cheshire cat smile and say "Your *ga* is a little flat," or "Maybe you just can't cut it." The opportunity to move with Viswa since 1983 as student, collaborator, and friend, is something I will treasure all my days.

Viswa and I planned to dedicate our book to his niece, Lakshmi Shanmukam Knight, and his cousin T. Sankaran, both of whom passed on in 2001. I hope he will not object if the book is also now dedicated to his living memory. Consummate performer, visionary educator, and dear friend, we miss you terribly. As you taught us, we carry on in your spirit. *Mika nanṟi*, Viswa.

M.H.A.
Norton, Massachusetts
10 July 2003

Contents

Foreword

In the past three decades interest in music around the world has surged, as evidenced in the proliferation of courses at the college level, the burgeoning "world music" market in the recording business, and the extent to which musical performance is evoked as a lure in the international tourist industry. This heightened interest has encouraged an explosion in ethnomusicological research and publication, including the production of reference works and textbooks. The original model for the "world music" course—if this is Tuesday, this must be Japan—has grown old, as has the format of textbooks for it, either a series of articles in single multiauthored volumes that subscribe to the idea of "a survey" and have created a canon of cultures for study, or single-authored studies purporting to cover world musics or ethnomusicology. The time has come for a change.

This Global Music Series offers a new paradigm. Instructors can now design their own courses; choosing from a set of case study volumes, they can decide which and how much music they will teach. The series also does something else; rather than uniformly taking a large region and giving superficial examples from several different countries within it, case studies offer two formats—some focused on a specific culture, some on a discrete geographical area. In either case, each volume offers greater depth than the usual survey. Themes significant in each instance guide the choice of music that is discussed. The contemporary musical situation is the point of departure in all the volumes, with historical information and traditions covered as they elucidate the present. In addition, a set of unifying topics such as gender, globalization, and authenticity occur throughout the series. These are addressed in the framing volume, *Thinking Musically* (Wade), which sets the stage for the case studies by introducing those topics and other ways to think about how people make music meaningful and useful in their lives. *Thinking Musically* also presents the basic elements of music as they are practiced in musical systems around the world so that authors of each case study do not have to spend time explaining them and can delve immediately into the particular music. A second framing volume, *Teaching Music Globally* (Campbell), guides teachers in the use of *Thinking Musically* and the case studies.

The series subtitle, "Experiencing Music, Expressing Culture," also puts in the forefront the people who make music or in some other way experience it and also through it express shared culture. This resonance with global studies in such disciplines as history and anthropology, with their focus on processes and themes that permit cross-study, occasions the title of this Global Music Series.

Bonnie C. Wade
Patricia Shehan Campbell
General Editors

Preface

We wrote this book with several types of reader in mind: the general reader who has an interest in South India, the student taking a course in world music or ethnomusicology, and the primary or secondary school teacher who wishes to introduce music of different cultures into his or her classroom. The book assumes no previous knowledge of South India or its music; one feature we hope will be useful to the reader with little exposure to India is the inclusion of indented, italicized text boxes placed throughout the book that give brief explanations of topics such as Hinduism, caste, and yoga.

Cross-cultural study offers the student the opportunity to appreciate new music and, perhaps equally important, to gain new perspectives on previously held experiences and conceptions of music. This volume of the Global Music Series introduces the reader to music and music makers in South India. The book's primary focus is on one of the great performance traditions in the world today, Karṇāṭak music. Known by South Indians as their classical art music tradition, Karṇāṭak music dives deep into the ocean of melody and rhythm. Someone looking for a systematic way of expanding her or his understanding of musical scale beyond the duality of major and minor, or of rhythm beyond the categories of duple or triple, need look no further. And in Karṇāṭak music, gorgeous musical compositions are brought into juxtaposition with an astounding array of different types of improvisation. As such, the study of South Indian music provides a potentially illuminating look at the pervasive assumption that composition and improvisation are inherently dissimilar, if not mutually exclusive, modes of musical activity.

Beyond the Karṇāṭak concert tradition, South India is home to many rich artistic environments. Selectively addressed in the book's final chapter, these include the thriving popular music scene (historically rooted in stage drama and, since the 1930s, the cinema), a myriad of regional music traditions traversing a continuum between sacred and secular (many of them integrating elements of dance and drama), and contemporary composition.

THEMES AND CONTENT

Woven throughout the fabric of the book are several themes, discussions that will help lead the reader to a deeper understanding of musical life in South India. As ethnomusicologists, we believe that social organization plays a central role in shaping the music we hear, not just its various contexts but the sounds themselves. Considerable attention has been given in this book to the histories of gender and caste relations in South India because, we would argue, without an understanding of these histories it is simply not possible to explain the profound changes that took place in South Indian musical performance in the twentieth century, generating the tradition as it exists today. A second theme is the interplay between the sometimes complementary and sometimes conflicting imperatives of devotion and virtuosity. The lyrics of Karṇāṭak compositions are almost all of a devotional nature and the great composers of the tradition are revered as saints. At the same time however, concert performance today is in many ways a secular world in which musicians are judged first and foremost on their professional skills, and compositions are scrutinized as works of art, appreciated for their sophisticated construction. A third theme rises from another dialectic between the concepts of improvisation and composition. The reverence accorded South Indian composers such as Tyagaraja, the central place held by compositions in Karṇāṭak music, and the premium placed on fidelity to the composition in performers' interpretations, are examined in light of the equally important appreciation of a musician's ability to display his or her creativity in performance, the wide range of improvisational genres used in Karṇāṭak music today, and the ways in which composition can be seen as flexible and improvisation as structured.

Of the book's five chapters, the first four are primarily concerned with the Karṇāṭak concert tradition. Chapter 1 focuses on song; it begins with analysis of a performance of *bhajan*, a structurally simple devotional song genre, then proceeds to the primary concert genre *kriti*, showing how the more complex *kriti* grew from simpler forms. Chapter 2 presents an analysis of *rāga* and *tāḷa*, the primary musical elements undergirding the Karṇāṭak music system, and models a pedagogical approach used by many South Indian teachers in the early phases of training students. Chapter 3 presents a concert performance of a *kriti* (including on the CD a full, uncut recording of over 28 minutes) showing how Karṇāṭak musicians weave together composed and improvised elements to create multichambered extended performances. Chapter 4 examines the evolution of music during the twentieth century with special attention to factors of gender and caste, illuminated through case studies (and historical recordings) of a small group of enormously influential musicians. Chapter 5 moves outside of the Karṇāṭak concert world to give an overview of other important South Indian musical forms and performance settings.

LEARNING AIDS

We have provided listening guides and activities throughout the text to help readers get the most out of both the text and the selections on the accompanying CD. Places in the text linked with a supplementary web listening guide or activity are clearly marked. Further material is provided on Oxford's accompanying website: www.oup.com/us/globalmusic. Additional listening guides and activities are also available at the author's website: www.wheatoncollege.edu/Faculty/MatthewAllen.html.

NOTE ON TRANSLITERATION AND PRONUNCIATION

Transliteration decisions are subjective and variously applied. We have rendered people's names as commonly spelled, without diacritical marks. Geographical terms, names of deities, languages, literary works, performance genres, and musical terms have been given diacritics. Names of genres, musical terms, and most other Indian language words are italicized, with the exception of the words Karṇāṭak (rendered by some authors as "Karnatic" or "Carnatic"), rāga, and tāḷa, due to the frequency with which they are used. When a word is used in the plural, it is given the English *–s* ending, italicized with the rest of the word. Names of many cities have recently been changed, and we have used the new designations such as Chennai, Mumbai, and Kolkata, rather than Madras, Bombay, and Calcutta.

Vowel length is indicated by a macron over the letter. The letter *a* is pronounced as the vowel "u" in "puppy," *e* as the "e" in "effort," *i* as in "pit," *o* as in "short," *u* as in "pull." Linger over long *ā, ē, ī, ō,* and *ū,* as in "call," "baby," "bee," "go," and "moon." The consonants *c* and *g* are as in "church" and "garb," never as "coat" and "page." *S* is as in "mustard," not "music." *Ś* and *ṣ* are slightly different renderings of "sh." *R* and the liquid Tamiḻ *ṟ* are pronounced similarly to the single-flap *r* of Spanish. Vocalic r (*ṛ*) is pronounced as *ri* in "rich." A dot under a consonant indicates retroflex; *ṭ, ḍ, ṇ,* and *ḷ* sound as if preceded by a hint of *r*—for example, *solkaṭṭu* sounds a bit like "solkarttu," *eḍuppu* like "erduppu," *caraṇam* like "cararnam," and *tāḷa* like "tārla." Consonants followed by *h* are aspirated, as with *t* and *p* in "hothouse" and "uphill." The voiced, retroflexed, frictionless continuant *ḻ* is pronounced somewhere between the sound of *r* and *zh,* as in *Tamiḻ* or *Cōḻa.* As a rule we have softened interior consonants to approximate pronounciation; for example, *padam* instead of the strict transliteration *patam.*

ACKNOWLEDGMENTS

We have many to thank for their help in bringing this collaborative book to life. A core group of colleagues has been with us since the inception of the project, responding to endless emails and manuscript drafts. James Cowdery, Rolf Groesbeck, Gayathri Rajapur Kassebaum, Douglas Knight, David Nelson, B. M. Sundaram, Bonnie Wade, Phillip Wagoner, Richard Wolf, and two anonymous readers have given our work the quality of attention and critical review that we can never adequately repay.

Crucial assistance was given with particular parts of the manuscript by R. Balasubramaniam, S. Theodore Baskaran, Frank Bennett, Bryan Burton, Joseph Getter, William Jackson, Viswanath Kaladharan, L. S. Rajagopalan, N. Ramanathan, V. A. K. Ranga Rao, Devesh Soneji, Yoshitaka Terada, C. M. Venkatachalam, Dominique Vitalyos, and Phillip Zarrilli. We have also benefited greatly from the contributions of Geetha Ramanathan Bennett, Patricia Sheehan Campbell, Amy Catlin, Christine Guillebaud, Parvathy Hadley, Guddappa Jogi and ensemble, S. Nagesh Kini, Michael Kinnear, Anantha Krishnan, Mike Lang, Usha Murali and ensemble, Harish Neelakandan, Shashikala Padaki, Maribeth Payne, S. V. Raman, Prasanna Ramaswamy, Lewis Rowell, George Ruckert, David Sanford, Trichy Sankaran, Zoe Sherinian, Sheenu Srinivasan, Jan Steward, Srivatsan Varadarajan, Venkat Venkataraman, Kiranavali Vidyasankar, and Amanda Weidman.

For graciously facilitating permissions, we are grateful to Jeffrey Aristy (Taylor and Francis Publishers), Cathy Carapella (Diamondtime, Ltd.), Alisa Cole (Narada Productions, Inc.), Yale Evelev (Luaka Bop,

Inc.), and Atesh Sonneborn (Smithsonian Folkways Recordings). For technical assistance, our thanks to audio engineers Rick Britto (Saurus Studio), Allan Evans (Arbiter Records) and Joe Patrych; George Hart, developer of the *timesindian* font; Christin Ronolder, director of visual resources in Wheaton College's art department, and Macintosh experts Ken Davignon and Morgan Holland.

I (Matthew) would like to acknowledge the American Institute of Indian Studies for a junior fellowship that allowed me to complete a year's dissertation research in Chennai in 1989–90, and in particular the counsel and friendship of Dr. Pappu Venugopal Rao, AIIS Associate Director General in Chennai, Dr. Shubha Chaudhuri, Director of the AIIS Archives and Research Centre for Ethnomusicology in Delhi, and Sri T. S. Parthasarathy and Smt. Nandini Ramani, eminent Secretaries of the Madras Music Academy. To all those who have befriended and educated me along this route go my deepest thanks: Julie, Kayla, and Emma; Viswa, Jody, Kumar, Jay, and Kerey; Ranga, Edwina, Sudhama and Arun; Doug, Lakshmi, Aniruddha, and Muni; Mukthamma, Sulochanamma, Brindamma and families; Sankaranna, S. Yadav Murti and family; V. Tyagarajan, V. Nagarajan and families; G. Saraswati, A. Sankaranarayan, Usha, Vidya, Ganesh, and Satish; Jayendran Pillay and family; B. M. Sundaram and family; Ramnad Raghavan and family; S. V. and Meera Seshadri; Trichy and Lalitha Sankaran; Vanaja and Viji Jeyaraman; S. Lakshmivarahan, Sundara Rajan, S. Narasinga Rao, and families; Annamalai, Ranganayaki Ayyangar, T. S. Balasubramanian, K. Banumathi, Jon Barlow, Martin Clayton, Marcie Frishman, Kathryn Hansen, Dorothea Hast and Stanley Scott, S. R. Janakiraman, Saskia Kersenboom, Srinivas Krishnan, James Lindholm, Madurai G. S. Mani, Avanthi Meduri, Vijaysri Mokkapati, Murthy, Kalanidhi Narayanan, Daniel and Arundhati Neuman, Michael Nixon, Lauren Paul, Indira Viswanathan Peterson, Regula Qureshi, Madhavi Rajagopalan, Savitri Rajan, Cre-A S. Ramakrishnan, N. Ravikiran, David Reck, S. Seetha, N. Shashikiran, David Shulman, Mark and Greta Slobin, Amrit Srinivasan, Karaikudi Subramanian, Samuel Sudananda, T. A. Sundarambal, and Richard Widdess. I'd also like to thank the following people at Oxford University Press: Jan Beatty, sponsoring editor for music, Talia Krohn, editorial assistant, and Lisa Grzan, production editor.

Jody Viswanathan has asked that on Viswa's behalf, their dear friends S. Guhan and Shantha Guhan, V. K. Narayana Menon, Harold Powers, and Samuel and Luise Scripps be recognized for their support of the family over many decades.

CD Track List

1 *bhajan:* "Destroyer of Demons/*Dānava Bhanjana.*" Composer unknown. Recorded April 22, 2000, Cleveland, Ohio, by C. M. Venkatachalam. Performed by a *bhajan* group organized by Usha Murali. Used by permission of the Aradhana Committee, Cleveland Tyagaraja Festival, R. Balasubramaniam, president.

2 "Explanation of South Indian names." Recited by T. Viswanathan.

3 *kriti:* "I Trusted You/*Unnai Nambinēn.*" Composed by Muttuttandavar (seventeenth century). Performed by T. Viswanathan, vocal; Anantha Krishnan, violin; David Nelson, *mridaṅgam.* Recorded in concert at Columbia University, New York, April 17, 2001. Used by permission of the artists.

4 "Exercise in *Ādi* Tāḷa, Three Speeds." Recited by Matthew Allen.

5 "Exercise in *Tiśra Tripuṭa* Tāḷa, Three Speeds." Recited by Matthew Allen.

6 "Exercise in *Tiśra Ēka* Tāḷa, Three Speeds." Recited by Matthew Allen.

7 "Exercise Combining Phrases in *Tiśra Ēka* Tāḷa, Third Speed." Recited by Matthew Allen.

8 "Kīravāṇi Rāga." Sung by T. Viswanathan.

9 "Kāpi Rāga." Sung by T. Viswanathan.

10 "Three Major Categories of *Gamaka,* Ornamentation, Demonstrated in Kīravāṇi Rāga." Sung by T. Viswanathan.

11 "Phrases in Kīravāṇi Rāga." Sung by T. Viswanathan.

12 "Phrases in Kāpi Rāga." Sung by T. Viswanathan.

13–17 "Main Piece" performance by T. Brinda, vocal; T. Viswanathan, flute; T. Ranganathan, *mridaṅgam.* House concert in Chennai, India, 1977. Used by permission.

13 "Kīravāṇi Rāga *Ālāpana.*"

14 *Kriti:* "If It Was to Happen/*Kaligiyuṇṭē.*" Composed by Tyagaraja (1767–1847).

15 "*Niraval.*"

16 "*Svara Kalpana.*"

17 "*Tani Āvarttanam*—Drum Solo."

18 *jāvaḷi:* "Didn't I Tell You Not To, Girl/*Vaddani?*" Composed by Mysore Venkatarama Sastri (nineteenth century). Performers: Bangalore Nagarathnammal, voice; violin and *mridaṅgam*, unknown. 78 RPM recording. His Master's Voice, Black label (Gramophone Company, India, Ltd.), disk P-5345. Recorded at Bangalore, December 1921; issued March 1923. Public domain.

19 "Scalar Summary and Phrases in Tōḍi Rāga." Sung by T. Viswanathan.

20 "*Ālāpana* in Tōḍi Rāga." Performed by T. N. Rajarattinam Pillai, *nāgasvaram.* 78 RPM recording. Odeon disk CA-720/1815, issued 1934. Public domain.

21 "Scalar Summary and Phrases in Sāvēri Rāga." Sung by T. Viswanathan.

22 *padam:* "No Matter How Often I Tell You/*Ettanai Connālum.*" Composed by Vaidisvarankoil Subbarama Ayyar (ca. 1830–1880). Performed by Ariyakkudi Ramanuja Ayyangar, voice; violin and *mridaṅgam,* unknown. 78 RPM recording. Odeon disk A102/MD 662, issued November 1932. Public domain.

23 "*Iḍakka,*" performed by P. M. Narayana Marar, from the recording *Music from South India: Kerala,* Folkways 4365, provided courtesy of Smithsonian Folkways Recordings. © 1961. Used by permission.

24 "*Naḷa Caritam,*" from the recording *Music from South India: Kerala,* Folkways 4365, provided courtesy of Smithsonian Folkways Recordings. © 1961. Used by permission. Performed by vocalists M. E. P. Pillai and Gopinathan Nayar, drummers K. Damodaran Pannikar and Vasudeva Poduwal, and actors (anklets can be heard jingling as they dance) Mankulam Vishnu Nambudiri and Kudamalur Karunakaran Nayar.

25 Cinema song: "When I Say Come/*Ba Ennalu.*" Music composed by Vijay Anand; lyrics composed by Chi Udayashanker. Sung by S. P. Balasubrahmanyam and Manjula Guru. From the CD *Asia Classics I:*

Dance Raja Dance, Luaka Bop 72438-49032-2-0, 1992. Used by permission of Narada Productions, Inc., o/b/o Luaka Bop, Inc. ℗ 1989 Sangeetha/The Master Recording Company.

26 *kriti:* "Can There Be Release/*Mōkṣamu Galadā*?" Composed by Tyagaraja (1767–1847). Performed by Geetha Ramanathan Bennett, voice; and Mike Lang, piano. Arrangement and performance © 2001, Frank Bennett. Used by permission.

27 *tatva:* "Why Do You Worry/*Yāke Cinti*?" Composed by Sharif Saheb (early twentieth century). Performed by Guddappa Jogi and N. Guddappa, voice; Gudeppa and Sivalingappa, harmonium, *tāḷam* cymbals, and responsorial singing. Recorded by Gayathri Rajapur Kassebaum. Used by permission of the artists.

CHAPTER 1

Song in South India

Śrī gaṇanātha sindhūra varṇa, karuṇa sāgara karivadana
O thou lord of Śiva's attendants (called Gaṇanātha or Gaṇēśa), with crimson body; ocean of compassion, with elephant face
(Refrain) Lambōdara lakumi kara, ambāsuta amaravinuta, lambōdara lakumi kara
O thou rotund Lord, giver of wealth (Lakṣmi), son of mother goddess (Ambā), worshiped by all the gods; O thou rotund Lord, giver of all wealth
Siddha cāraṇa gaṇa sēvita, siddhi vināyaka tē namō namō (lambōdara . . .)
You are propitiated by sages (siddha), by those who have attained completeness; O remover of obstacles, I bow to you (O thou rotund lord . . .)
Sakala vidya ādi pūjita, sarvottama tē namō namō (lambōdara . . .)
To you are offered prayers (pūja) before beginning any undertaking; O thou most perfect Lord, I bow to you (O thou rotund lord . . .)

—*Śrī Gaṇanātha, Kannada language gītam by Purandara Dāsa (1484–1564), by tradition the first song taught to Karṇāṭak music students*

BHAJAN (DEVOTIONAL SONG)

On a cold gray morning in late April, a piercing wind whips in off Lake Erie. Several hundred people of South Indian descent who have come from across the United States and Canada hurry into a hall at Cleveland State University, wearing heavy winter coats over their light cotton *dhōtis* and gold-bordered silk *sāris*. They are drawn to this most un–South Indian climate for the *ārādhana*, the annual festival honoring South India's most beloved composer, Tyagaraja (1767–1847). The celebration in Cleveland, just as those now taking place in many cities around the world with a sizeable South Indian population, brings el-

FIGURE 1.1 *Bronze statuette, dancing* Gaṇēśa. *(Photograph by Matthew Allen)*

ders thoughts of home while educating young South Indians growing up in the diaspora about their ancestral heritage.

At the festival a range of performances takes place, including evening music and dance concerts by visiting professional performers and many shorter presentations by young students or adult amateurs, all intent upon paying musical homage to the venerated composer. CD track 1, "Destroyer of Demons/*Dānava Bhanjana,*" was recorded at the opening Saturday morning session of the Cleveland Tyagaraja celebration on April 22, 2000. After Brahmin Hindu priests performed appropriate *pūjas*, religious rituals, several groups of local musicians sang devotional

LATEST INVENTION!
The only Perfect instrument for culture of
SOUTH INDIAN MUSIC.
"GOLD MEDAL"
HARMONIUM
Style No. 7—3 oct.
single Paris Kasriel reed
Rs. 45
Style No. 8—3 oct.
double Paris Kasriel reed.
Rs. 75
Order with Rs. 10 advance.
Special Terms—Delivery Free for Full Amount in Advance.
NATIONAL HARMONIUM CO.,
8a Lalbazar Street, CALCUTTA.

FIGURE 1.2 *Harmonium advertisement,* The Hindu, *Chennai (Madras), January 29, 1930.* (Courtesy of Matthew Allen)

songs called *bhajans*. One of the groups consisted of eight singers and instrumentalists organized for the festival by Usha Murali. The young girl singing the lead role on this song, Arthi Narayanan, sat in the middle of the stage, flanked by three supporting singers who clapped in time to the rhythm during the second half of the song. Sitting in back of the singers and providing rhythmic accompaniment were three drummers—one player of the *ḍhōlak*, a double-headed membranophone popular in many Indian folk music traditions, and two performers on the *kañjīra*, a tambourine-like small frame drum with metal jingles attached to its wooden shell. A young man sitting with the singers provided melodic accompaniment on a portable keyboard instrument called a *harmonium*—an instrument of European origin with a chequered history in India.

∞

The Harmonium in India—loved and reviled. *This portable bellows-operated aerophone was introduced into India by Christian missionaries approximately two centuries ago. As a fixed keyboard instrument, it cannot produce microtones or the subtle nuances of Indian vocal ornamentation, leading many people to consider it unfit for Indian music. Despite its limitations, however, it has become extremely popular, especially for accompaniment. Today it is the most commonly used melodic accompaniment instrument in North Indian* Hindustāni *music and is very popular in* bhajan *groups in South India. Before an intense campaign to ban it from the concert stage and radio in the 1930s, it was beginning to gain significant popularity in* Karṇāṭak *(sometimes spelled* Karnatic *or* Carnatic*) art music as well. Figure 1.2, an advertisement from the Chennai newspaper* The Hindu, *offers a rather fancy harmonium to the public; note that the manufacturer placing the ad is not from the South but rather from the northeastern city of Calcutta (now Kolkata).*

Songs and Singing. This first chapter focuses on song—an artifact of human expression combining words and music—for two reasons. First, song is familiar in many cultures, a basic way in which billions of people organize sound and communicate musically. Study of song can serve as a bridge for beginning to cross cultural boundaries. Second, in the South Indian *Karṇāṭak* concert music tradition, songs form a composed core around which several types of improvisations are built. South Indian vocal *and* instrumental music performance is almost always based upon song, that is, upon music that has been set to a text. If you hear a South Indian flute or violin concert, you can be confident that the instrumentalists are drawing from the same stock of songs that you'd hear in a vocal concert. While not all instrumentalists know the words to the songs they play, many do, and playing an instrument in a *gāyaki,* or "singing," style is highly valued. Understanding the song at the core of a performance, then, is a vital first step to understanding the whole performance.

ACTIVITIES 1.1–1.3 Bhajan: *"Destroyer of Demons/* Dānava Bhanjana" *(CD Track 1)*

Listen to the bhajan *while using the translation and listening guide that follow. As you listen, try pronouncing the words and following the progress through the text over the course of the performance. Then, write down your first impressions of the performance. For example, note repetition of melodic lines; at what points the melody rises and falls in range or dynamic level; changes of tempo or general "energy level" during the performance; the vocal quality of the singers; and what categories of instruments you can hear performing—chordophone, membranophone, aerophone, or idiophone. The four text lines of the* bhajan *are labeled* A–D *to facilitate reference to the listening guide. Each line of the* bhajan *is sung first by the solo singer, then repeated by the group. This call-and-response structure, building energy through repetition and dialogue, is typical of* bhajan *performance. In the slower first section (Activity 1.2), most lines of the song are repeated.*

ACTIVITY 1.1 *Text and Translation*

(A) *Dānava bhanjana rāma sāyī śyāmaḷa kōmaḷa rām*	Destroyer of demons, Rāma Sāyī, dark hued, soft and sweet Rāma
(B) *Hē rāma rāma jaya rāma sāyī rāma rāma rām*	Oh Rāma Rāma, victorious Rāma Sāyī, Rāma Rāma Rām
(C) *Dasaratha nandana rāma sāyī daya sāgara rām*	Son of Dasaratha, Rāma Sāyī, ocean of compassion, Rām
(D) *He dīnom kē prabhū rāma sāyī rāma rāma rām*	Oh lord and protector, Rāma Sāyī, Rāma Rāma Ram

[Translated from the Sanskrit and Hindi by C. M. Venkatachalam]

ACTIVITY 1.2 *Listening Guide Part 1: Slow First Section*

Time	Melodic range	Performance notes	Text line
0:00		*Harmonium intro*	
0:05	Low	Leader sings	(A) *Dānava bhanjana rāma sāyī śyāmaḷa kōmaḷa rām*
0:14	Low	Choral response	(drummers enter at this point)
0:22	Low	Leader, then chorus	(A) *Dānava bhanjana rāma sāyī śyāmaḷa kōmaḷa rām*
0:39	Middle	Leader, then chorus	(B) *Hē rāma rāma jaya rāma sāyī rāma rāma rām*
0:56	Middle	Leader, then chorus	(B) *Hē rāma rāma jaya rāma sāyī rāma rāma rām*
1:12	Low	Leader, then chorus (drummers pause)	(A) *Dānava bhanjana rāma sāyī śyāmaḷa kōmaḷa rām*
1:29	High	Leader, then chorus	(C) *Dasaratha nandana rāma sāyī daya sāgara rām*
1:46	High	Leader, then chorus	(C) *Dasaratha nandana rāma sāyī daya sāgara rām*
2:02	Middle	Leader, then chorus	(D) *He dīnom kē prabhū rāma sāyī rāma rāma rām*
2:18	Middle	Leader, then chorus	(D) *He dīnom kē prabhū rāma sāyī rāma rāma rām*

After the fourth line is complete, the lead singer returns to the first line, beginning the faster second section (Activity 1.3). The group starts through the entire form again, this time without as many repeats. Can you feel the tempo and energy pick up at this point (approximately 2:35 into the performance)? The energetic handclaps that also begin at this point complement the acceleration of tempo by the drummers. At the end of the fast section the percussionists drop out and the vocalists sing the first line of text once more, ending the bhajan. *At this point the harmonium introduces the next* bhajan *and the lead singer (this time a man) begins to sing its first line. This segue is typical of* bhajan *sessions, which often include many songs in succession.*

ACTIVITY 1.3 *Listening Guide Part 2: Faster Second Section*

Time	Melodic range	Performance notes	Text line
		(Clapping begins and tempo increases)	
2:35	Low	Leader, then chorus	(A) *Dānava bhanjana rāma* *sāyī śyāmaḷa kōmaḷa rām*
2:49	Middle	Leader, then chorus	(B) *Hē rāma rāma jaya rāma* *sāyī rāma rāma rām*
3:04	Low	Leader, then chorus	(A) *Dānava bhanjana rāma* *sāyī śyāmaḷa kōmaḷa rām*
3:18	High	Leader, then chorus	(C) *Dasaratha nandana rāma* *sāyī daya sāgara rām*
3:33	Middle	Leader, then chorus	(D) *He dīnom kē prabhū* *rāma sāyī rāma rāma rām*
3:47	Middle	Leader, then chorus	(D) *He dīnom kē prabhū* *rāma sāyī rāma rāma rām*
4:02	Low	All sing together, percussionists stop	(A) *Dānava bhanjana rāma* *sāyī śyāmaḷa kōmaḷa rām*
4:10			(Transition to next bhajan . . .)

Meaning of the Text: Devotion, Love, and Praise. The words *bhajan* (devotional song) and *bhakti* (devotional love) both come from the Sanskrit word root *bhaj,* to worship or praise. As you listened, perhaps you noted that the group kept coming back to one word throughout—the name of the Hindu deity Rāma (often pronounced, as on CD track 1, as "Rām").

∞

Hinduism and chanting the names of god. *The estimated population of India as of July 2002 is 1,045,845,000; approximately 820 million Indian citizens are Hindus, while 120 million practice Islam, 23 million are Christian, 19 million are Sikh, and approximately 25 million are Buddhist,*

Jain, or Parsi. Hindu scriptures are broadly classified as either śruti, *"heard," or* smriti, *"remembered." The oldest texts, the* Vēdas, *constitute śruti, containing sacred syllables* (mantras) *believed to have been heard directly by early sages. The aphoristic* Upaniṣads, *expositions by teachers to their students on the philosophical essence of the* Vēdas, *are also considered* śruti. *Works remembered and written down,* smriti, *include the epics* Rāmāyaṇa *and* Mahābhārata *(the stories of Rāma and* Kṛṣṇa, *respectively), and the moral stories known as* Purāṇas.

While in Hindu practice many forms of deity are recognized, and while Hindus normally take a particular god or goddess to be their personal deity, the many deities are generally viewed as providing different paths to the same godhead. Among the most widely worshiped are the god Viṣṇu, together with two of his ten incarnations, Rāma and Kṛṣṇa; the god Śiva in his many forms (including Naṭarāja, discussed later in this chapter) and his two sons Gaṇēśa and Murugan; and the goddess in one of her many manifestations. Sarasvatī, Lakṣmī, and Pārvatī, considered the spouses of Brahmā, Viṣṇu, and Śiva, respectively, and collectively referred to as Śakti, Ambā, or Dēvī, attract many millions of devotees.

Repeated chanting or singing of the name of gods and goddesses, as heard in CD track 1, is an important Hindu worship practice (Raghavan 1994). Many North Americans and Europeans now in their thirties or older heard this practice for the first time in the chanting of saffron-robed Hare Kṛṣṇas; *just one of many sects of Kṛṣṇa devotees, they gained wide visibility outside India by establishing centers in major world cities beginning in the 1960s.*

∞

Rāma, stoic protagonist of the epic *Rāmāyaṇa,* and the perpetually youthful, virile, and playful flute-playing deity Kṛṣṇa, are two of the ten incarnations of the deity Viṣṇu. "Destroyer of demons" describes Rāma's heroic and virtuous attributes—he is the victorious slayer of demons, an ocean of compassion, and protector of his devotees. Rāma is who the composer Tyagaraja chose as his personal deity and addressed in most of his songs. The word "Sāyī" appended to the name of Rāma at several places in the text is a reference to Śrī Sathya Sāyī Bāba, spiritual *guru* or guide to the members of this performing group. The *bhajan* group thus pays homage simultaneously to Tyagaraja, the Hindu deity Rāma, and their living spiritual guide Sāyī Bāba.

Celebrating Tyagaraja in the United States and in South India. The Cleveland celebration is a good example of how immigrants to the United States transplant and adapt cultural forms from their homelands to a new environment. In 1978 a small group of South Indian families, inspired by Karṇāṭak drummer Ramnad Raghavan and including R. Balasubramaniam (known as "Cleveland Balu"), Gomathy Balu, V. V. Sundaram, Toronto Venkataraman, and the late Professor T. Temple Tuttle of Cleveland State University, started a yearly festival to commemorate Tyagaraja's life and work. Over the last twenty-five years, the Cleveland Tyagaraja festival has grown to become the largest such commemoration in North America. This small group of South Indian immigrants to the United States patterned the activities after a celebration that has taken place each winter (usually early January) since 1907 in the small town of Tiruvaiyāṟu, seven or eight miles from the city of Tañjāvūr in the state of Tamiḻ Nāḍu (see Figure 1.3).

"Reading" South Indian names. *In South India people generally do not use a first–middle–last name format. While there is no one formula, it is common for a person to put first the name of his or her* ūr, *ancestral or home place (as Indians move abroad, this practice continues in names like "Cleveland Balu"). In some cases an honorific prefix, the name of a musician's instrument, or even a rāga with which a musician is strongly associated may substitute for the place name. Long names are often abbreviated to an initial. This first name is often followed by the given name of the birth or adoptive father (in some* dēvadāsi *families, as discussed in Chapter 4, the mother), then the person's given name. Until the mid-twentieth century, it was common to follow the given name with another term that indicated the caste (hereditary social community; see discussion later this chapter) of the person, but this practice has largely fallen out of use. Figure 1.4 (CD track 2) explains the names of some musicians mentioned in the book.*

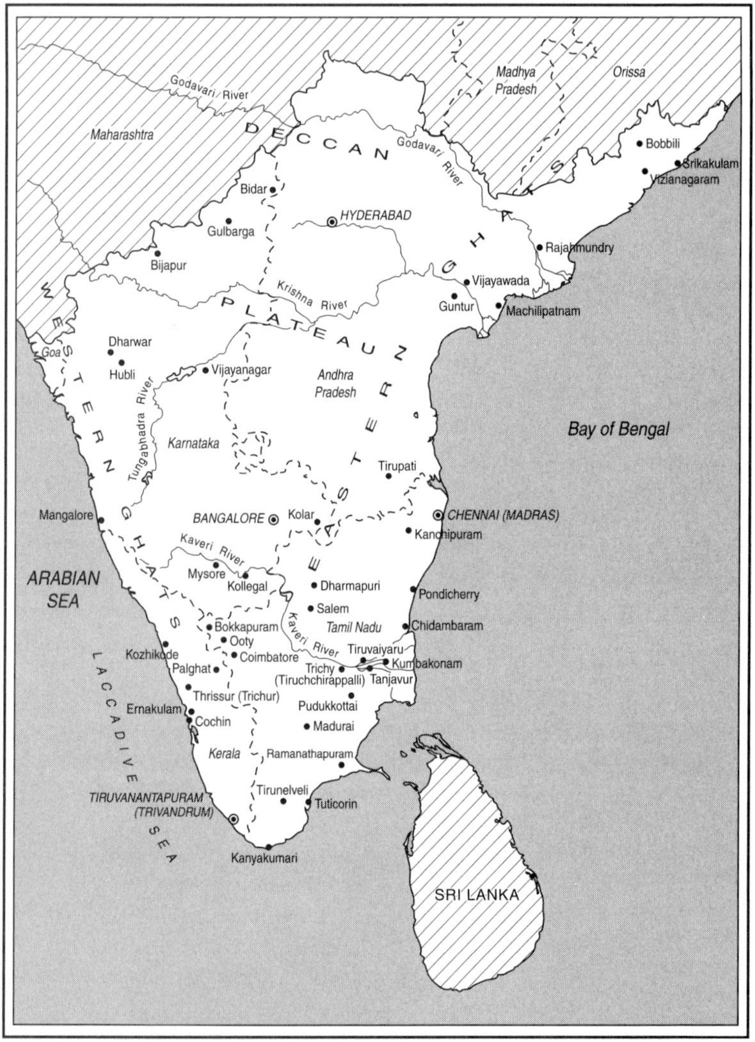

FIGURE 1.3 *South India. (© 2000. From "South Asia: The Indian Subcontinent," in Garland Encyclopedia of World Music, ed. Alison Arnold. Reproduced by permission of Routledge, Inc., part of The Taylor and Francis Group)*

Bangalore Nagarathnammal, Tanjavur Brinda: the ancestral place, followed by given name

Vina Dhanammal: the instrument she played, followed by her given name

Madurai Shanmukavadivu Subbulakshmi: ancestral place, mother's given name (the "elegant beauty" of Shanmuka, another name for Murugan), and her given name

Maha Vaidyanatha Ayyar: honorific prefix (Maha—"great"), given name (*Vaidyanatha* is a name for Śiva as healer), followed by *Ayyar* (Smarta Brahmin caste suffix)

Coimbatore Raghava Ayyar: his ancestral place, given name (*Raghava* is a name of Rāma), and caste suffix

Tiruvavadudurai Natesa Rajarattinam Pillai: his ancestral place, name of his adoptive father (his uncle), his given name (*Rajarattinam*—"king–jewel"), and *Pillai*, respectful caste suffix used by many male non-Brahmin musicians

Ariyakkudi Ramanuja Ayyangar: ancestral place (also his nickname), given name (*Ramanuja* was an eleventh-century A.D. Vaiṣṇavite philosopher), *Ayyangar* (Vaiṣṇava Brahmin caste suffix)

Kancipuram Nayana Pillai: ancestral place, his nickname (*Nayana*—"darling"; his birth name was Subramania, one of the sons of Śiva), and caste suffix

FIGURE 1.4 *Explanation of South Indian names* *(CD track 2)*

Tiruvaiyāṟu (Figure 1.5) is located at the confluence of several branches of the Kāvēri river system, in the middle of the richest rice-growing district in the South. Because of the agricultural wealth of the region, the Kāvēri delta was for many centuries the center of South Indian political dynasties, until the European powers established their hegemony during the eighteenth and nineteenth centuries. Towns and villages throughout the countryside are studded with magnificent Hindu temples (Figures 1.6 and 1.7), evidence of past Rājas' munificent patronage of religion and the arts. This lush green environment is the place where Tyagaraja lived his life, composed and sang hundreds of devotional songs to his personal deity Rāma, and taught his many students.

After Tyagaraja's death his musical disciples began the practice of honoring their teacher, getting together and singing a few of his songs on the anniversary of his death (Sankaran and Allen in Arnold 2000: 383–396). Over time the commemoration evolved slowly into a bigger,

FIGURE 1.5 *Houses built by the Rāja of Tañjāvūr for Brahmin residents of Tiruvaiyāṟu, Tañjāvūr District.* (*Courtesy of T. Sankaran*)

more public affair, combining several types of musical performance with various domestic and religious ritual observances honoring the composer. Today thousands of people pour into the small town for the festival, alongside the technicians of All India Radio and the satellite-carrying semi trucks of Doordarshan, the Indian national television. Those who cannot make the trip from the state capitol Chennai (under the British called Madras) two hundred miles to the northeast—or from Mumbai (Bombay), Delhi, or Kolkata (Calcutta)—can tune in to the sights and sounds of the festival from their living rooms at home.

Languages of the Region. "Destroyer of Demons/*Dānava Bhanjana*" is primarily in the Sanskrit language, and also contains one phrase (dīnom kē prabhū) in Hindi. South India is an intensely multilingual environment, many residents speaking two or more languages fluently.

FIGURE 1.6 *Sārangapāṇi Viṣṇu temple complex, with Pothamarai* kuḷam *temple tank in foreground, Kumbakōṇam, Tañjāvūr District.* (Courtesy of David Sanford)

The indigenous languages of the South belong to the Dravidian language group. Some tribal people in isolated areas of North India also speak Dravidian languages, leading scholars to believe that Dravidian-speaking people once occupied a much greater area of the subcontinent. Soon after India's independence from Britain in 1947, most of the newly created states were organized on a linguistic basis, so that today each of the four states of southern India has an official, Dravidian, language. These languages—Tamiḻ (in Tamiḻ Nāḍu state), Telugu (Āndhra Pradesh), Malayāḷam (Kēraḷa), and Kannaḍa (Karṇāṭaka)—are structurally related but not mutually intelligible. The oldest language of the group, Tamiḻ, has a vast literature going back at least two millennia to legendary *Saṅgams*, academies, which supported poets and literary scholars (Ramanujan 1985).

The Dravidian languages are distinct from the Indo-Aryan group to which most North Indian and many European languages belong. Sanskrit—the ancient Indo-Aryan language in which the *Vēdas*, the epics *Rāmāyaṇa* and *Mahābhārata*, and a great body of dramatic literature and poetry are composed—is not a spoken language today, but many South

FIGURE 1.7 *Brahmadēśa Śiva temple, near Cheramadevi, Tirunelvēli District. (Courtesy of David Sanford)*

Indian composers have set their compositions in Sanskrit. The most widely spoken contemporary Indo-Aryan language of North India, Hindi, is learned by many South Indians but rarely spoken as a mother tongue. Further complicating the linguistic picture, the language of the former colonial power, English, remains extremely important in South India today as a link language enabling people of different mother tongues to communicate, and as a medium for scholarly writing and creative expression (as examples of creative writing on music in English, see Narayan 1982, Jairazbhoy 1991, Roy 1997).

KRITI

Evolution of Kriti. The next genre of composition to be considered, *kriti* (from the Indo-Aryan word root *kṛ*, "to create"), is structurally more complex than *bhajan*. The *kriti* has three distinct sections; it evolved from earlier South Indian genres such as the *saṅkīrtanam*, which had two sections, a *pallavi*, sprouting, and one or more *caraṇams*, stanzas (literally, "feet"). In *saṅkīrtanam*, the *pallavi* (labeled A) is sung first; then, after singing successive *caraṇams* (B1, B2, etc.), the singer returns to a brief restatement of the *pallavi* (A′). The *saṅkīrtanam* form came to fruition in the compositions of the Telugu composer Tallapaka Annamacarya (1424–1503).

A	B1	A′	B2	A′	(etc.)
Pallavi	Caraṇam 1	Pallavi reprise	Caraṇam 2	Pallavi reprise	

Note: a performance moves in time from left to right

During the sixteenth or perhaps seventeenth century, composers started to add a third section called *anupallavi*, literally, "continuation of the sprouting," placing it between *pallavi* and *caraṇam*. This crucial innovation created the *kriti*. The *pallavi* section continued to serve as a theme of return. The basic form of *kriti* in performance is therefore:

A	B	A′	C	A′
Pallavi	Anupallavi	Pallavi reprise	Caraṇam	Pallavi reprise

Many early *kritis* contained multiple *caraṇams*, like *saṅkīrtanams*, but in concerts today usually only one *caraṇam* is performed.

Text and Context—a Continuum of Performance from Devotion to Virtuosity. Like *bhajans*, the texts of *kritis* are devotional, but while *bhajans* are almost always performed in an explicitly devotional context (for a detailed account of *bhajan* performance in Chennai, see Singer 1972:199–241), *kritis* are performed in a wider variety of situations. The court at Tañjāvūr supported many artists including Tyagaraja's father, who was patronized by the Rāja for his discourses on the *Rāmāyaṇa*. Tyagaraja himself, however, is believed to have completely rejected any kind of patronage, refusing to sing before would-be royal or merchant patrons. He preferred to pour out his devotional *kritis* to Rāma in the privacy of his own worship or for his large group of musical disciples. It is important to remember that in Tyagaraja's lifetime, the public music concert—where a would-be listener buys a ticket and takes a seat in an auditorium—did not exist. One major performance context for Tyagaraja and his disciples was the *uñcavritti bhajana*. This involved going from house to house singing devotional songs and accepting rice and vegetables offered by the people, who regarded Tyagaraja and his disciples as devotees of Rāma and their visit to the neighborhood as a blessing. Since Tyagaraja's day the performance of *kritis* has gradually moved outward from the devotional context to encompass more secular, virtuosic performance contexts. Musicians of later generations, while venerating Tyagaraja's and other composers' devotional compositions, took them beyond a strictly devotional context into a "classical" performance tradition involving concert halls, audio recordings, and international tours. Today's professional musicians look for compositions that give what they call "scope" to demonstrate the depth of the musical system and to provide outlets for their virtuosity and creativity. To achieve these goals, *kritis* are overwhelmingly the genre of choice in Karṇāṭak concerts today.

What "classical" means in Indian music. *Karṇāṭak musicians today consider their music South India's "classical" music tradition, and in some ways—such as the importance given to compositions and the reverence in which great composers are held—the practice of Karṇāṭak music resembles that of European classical concert music. It is important, however, to note that some of the resonances that a connoisseur of Beethoven or Mozart would attach to the term do not apply in South India. Important differences in the two concepts of classical are that Karṇāṭak music contains extensive improvisation, its compositions are learned by rote and memorized by ear, and South Indian musicians do not play from written scores. To South Indians, calling Karṇāṭak music "classical" expresses the feeling that it is beautiful, sophisticated, systematic, sacred, and time-honored (one of the meanings of the term Karṇāṭak is "old").*

It is also important to note that the presentation and perception of Karṇāṭak music as "classical" today are the result of not only musical processes but also, crucially, of social and historical processes including profound changes in education and patronage under British colonial rule, the evolution of technology, massive migration from rural areas toward Chen-

nai and other cities, regional linguistic and political movements, and the Indian nationalist movement (see the discussion in Chapter 4). Also, Karṇāṭak music makes up only one small part of the total spectrum of musical performance in South India (on folk, tribal, Christian, and Muslim musical traditions, see Claus et al. 2002; Groesbeck and Palackal in Arnold 2000:929–951; Palackal 2001; Sherinian 2002; Wolf and Sherinian in Arnold 2000:903–928; Wolf 2001).

There are areas of overlap between the *kriti* and *bhajan*; some *kritis* are performed congregationally by *bhajan* groups, and a *bhajan* or another "light" piece may be performed at the end of a Karṇāṭak concert. The body of work of Tyagaraja himself illustrates this overlapping; while many of his lengthy, majestic *kritis* are at the heart of the Karṇāṭak concert repertoire today, some of his musically simpler compositions—often called *kīrtanas*, partly to distinguish them from concert *kritis*—are heard today in devotional settings:

> Songs in praise of divine names, *divyanāma kīrtanas*, consist of vocatives or dithyrambs, holy names which call to mind the Lord's actions and features. *Utsava sampradāya* songs are festive pieces celebrating the deity in a series of worshipful acts; waking, making offerings of milk and so on, swinging, celebrating marriage, singing lullabies. . . . *Kīrtanas* of the *divyanāma* and *utsava sampradāya* variety are better suited to group singing than *kritis*, which are more demanding and are often best sung by an individual after long hours of practice. Tyagaraja was not given to artistic snobbery, and composed great songs in both forms. (Jackson 1991:136)

A continuum may be sketched where on one extreme the focus of a performance is devotional and on the other, virtuosic, placing *bhajan* and *kriti* along this spectrum.

Devotion . . . tending toward group expression in home or temple, amateur performance	←→	*Virtuosity* . . . tending toward individual expression in public, professional performance

← *bhajan* →

← *kriti* →

In addition to differences in musical structure between *bhajan* and *kriti*, several other intertwined factors are at play that result in a difference in perception of their performance settings.

Professionalism: Karṇāṭak concert artists often depend on musical performance for at least part of their living, while *bhajan* singing groups are made up primarily of musical amateurs.

Group size: A *bhajan* session may involve just a few people in a private home but is often a larger group with several vocalists singing in call-and-response fashion. A Karṇāṭak performance (CD track 3) typically is a very intimate dialogue among a small group of three to five musicians.

Performer roles: Unlike the *bhajan* group, the Karṇāṭak performing ensemble itself generates a focus on one or perhaps two main artists, sitting in the center of the stage leading the ensemble, flanked by melodic and rhythmic accompanists.

Focus on music over text: There is an ongoing debate in South India among lovers of Karṇāṭak music about the importance of text vis-à-vis music. While the devotional nature and the artistry of the *kriti* texts—inheritors of a long tradition of devotional poetry—are treasured, many music lovers argue that the attention of the listener in a Karṇāṭak concert should be more on music than text, valorizing the experience of musical sound itself as a form of *yōga*. This *nāda yōga* (*yōga* of sound, *nāda*), free of attention to words, is for many listeners the raison d'être of the Karṇāṭak classical concert.

∞

Yōga *is a word many non-Indians are familiar with in one of its specific senses, a form of physical and spiritual discipline, a source of exercise and relaxation as well as spiritual uplift. The word comes from the same Indo-Aryan root as the English word* yoke *and in the Indian context is used for a variety of practices that share the common goal of uniting with (yoking to) the divine.* Nāda yōga *as a term for music embodies the idea that the experience of musical sound is a direct means of becoming united with the divine.*

∞

The *kriti* is a marvelously *flexible* genre of music. Depending on context, it slides along a scale between devotion and virtuosity. It may be performed relatively concisely and "no-frills," or it may be used by musicians as the basis for a virtuoso tour de force performance. The *kriti* to be considered later in this chapter, "I Trusted You/*Unnai Nambinēn,*" is rendered by the musicians in under three minutes in CD track 3. By contrast, Chapter 3 will demonstrate how a *kriti* can become the core of an almost half-hour-long performance in a concert situation.

Music, Language, and Politics. As in so many places around the world, language in South India is intimately intertwined with nation and region, with class, power, and status. The history of language use in South Indian music reflects the migrations of peoples from throughout the subcontinent into the area and the sociopolitical dynamics of the region. Tañjāvūr District in today's Tamiḻ Nāḍu state (Figure 1.3), the region where Tyagaraja lived, is in the heart of the Tamiḻ linguistic area. The rulers of Tañjāvūr from the sixteenth to nineteenth centuries did not speak Tamiḻ, however. They came as immigrants, first from Telugu-speaking, and later Marāṭhī-speaking, areas (Mahārāṣṭra is a state in west-central India). Although living in the Tamiḻ-speaking region, and despite a long heritage of songs and poetry composed in Tamiḻ, these rulers gave their patronage more to Sanskrit and Telugu than to Tamiḻ. The three most important composers of the late eighteenth through mid-nineteenth centuries, known to posterity as the *Trīmūrti* (Trinity)—Syama Sastri (1762–1827), Tyagaraja, and Muttusvami Dikshitar (1776–1835)—composed their *kritis* almost exclusively in Sanskrit and Telugu, not Tamiḻ. Patronage of Sanskrit and Telugu continued into the twentieth century as Karṇāṭak music moved from the extinct royal courts and vanishing private salons to the new public stage. Arts organizations in Chennai called *sabhās* started presenting Karṇāṭak music in a concert setting for the public in the early twentieth century, and by 1930 the seeds of today's thriving Karṇāṭak art music culture were in place, with most all compositions being sung in Telugu or Sanskrit.

The Tamiḻ Music Movement. In the early 1930s few of the songs performed in public concerts in Chennai were in Tamiḻ, the mother tongue of the majority of residents. A group of musicians, intellectuals, and philanthropists began agitating to have more Tamiḻ pieces performed in concerts and more recognition given to Tamiḻ composers. They argued that many good Tamiḻ songs were languishing for lack of respect and patronage. This argument was met by an opposing response to the effect that while no linguistic slight was intended, most Tamiḻ songs were simply musically inferior, and linguistic affirmative action should not be admitted into music. A heated and protracted controversy quickly developed partly because, for many people, social dynamics of caste and class lay not far below the surface of the musical argument. The debate over Tamil̲ music took on additional communal overtones because at this same time period the Self-Respect Movement, led by the non-Brahmin political leader E. V. Ramaswami Naicker, was revolutionizing the political terrain in Tamil̲ Nāḍu (Dirks 2001:257–265).

∞

Caste in South India. *The word caste is an Anglicization of the Portuguese casta, "lineage" or "breed." Theoretically, India's indigenous system of social organization consists of four overarching hereditarily determined social categories called* varṇa, *"color," each containing many* jātis, *"varieties," which Europeans came to translate with the term caste. The four* varṇas *and their affiliated, extremely generic, occupational practices are: Brahmins, who are priests and teachers;* kṣatriyas, *warriors and rulers;* vaiśyas, *farmers, merchants, or artisans; and* śudras, *laborers. The first three* varṇas *are known as "twice-born," whose males were historically eligible to learn Sanskrit, study the* Vēdas, *and perform rituals after a ceremony constituting a "second birth" (a very general comparison could be made to confirmation in the Roman Catholic church). Outside the four-*varṇa *system and at the very bottom of the social scale existed, and exists, a large segment of the population—perhaps as high as twenty percent in Tamil̲ Nāḍu—formerly called "untouchables" and today designated "Scheduled Castes,"* Dālits, *or* Ādi drāviḍa *(literally "first Dravidian," i.e., original inhabitant), living in conditions of extreme poverty. Most scholars feel that the theoretical four-varṇa system does not accurately describe South Indian society, where "today the Hindus divide themselves into three broad categories of castes: Brahman, non-Brahman and Ādi Drāviḍa" (Gough 1971:16).*

∞

The issue of caste relations is perhaps the most sensitive and contentious that the student of South Indian culture will encounter. The several branches of the upper caste Brahmin community in South

India, amounting to approximately five to seven percent of the population, have a long and distinguished history of scholarship, artistic achievement, philanthropy, and business acumen. The three great composers of the Trinity were Brahmins, for example, as have been many of the greatest South Indian musicians. Because of their birth into this social community, for centuries Brahmin South Indians received religious, social, and sometimes material benefits denied to members of other caste groups, a history that has had enduring acrimonious consequences for social relations between castes. In the arguments over whether and how to increase the profile of Tamiḻ music, many South Indians saw the denial of the value of Tamiḻ songs as a coded attack on non-Brahmin Tamiḻians. The fact that many of the most prominent supporters of Tamiḻ music—and critics of the inequities of the caste system (see the discussion of the film *Thyāgabhūmi* in Chapter 5)—have themselves been Brahmin only underscores the volatile emotions that inflamed this issue in the 1930s and still smolder today.

A wealthy banker from the non-Brahmin *Ceṭṭiyār* community, Annamalai Chettiar, provided the financial support giving the *Tamiḻ Iśai* (Tamiḻ Music) Movement its impetus. In 1929 he founded Minakshi College at Cidambaram, which later became Annamalai University; in the 1930s he endowed a music school there, and in the early 1940s the school instituted a new academic degree program centered on Tamiḻ music, the first in South India. In 1943 he founded the *Tamiḻ Iśai Sangam* (Tamiḻ Music Academy) in Chennai to promote the scholarly study and performance of Tamiḻ music. These institutions commissioned musicians to write new musical compositions in Tamiḻ, and—foreshadowing CD track 3—to compose new music for old Tamiḻ *kritis* whose musical settings had been forgotten. The financial incentives provided by Annamalai Chettiar and his colleagues, together with the efforts of musicians and intellectuals, spawned a renaissance of Tamiḻ music in its home state. As a result, today Tamiḻ songs are performed in most Karṇāṭak concerts, although the *kritis* of the Trinity—especially Tyagaraja's Telugu songs—remain the most performed concert works.

Muttuttandavar (Seventeenth Century). Muttuttandavar was the earliest important composer of Tamiḻ language *kritis*. Sources indicate that he belonged to a non-Brahmin caste of hereditary temple musicians who played ritual music in the *periya mēḷam*, "great ensemble." The instruments of this ensemble are the double-reed aerophone *nāgasvaram*, the double-headed membranophone *tavil*, *tāḷam* hand cymbals, and *śruti*

FIGURE 1.8 *Śiva Naṭarāja as king of dance. Tañjāvūr art plate by S. V. Raman. (Photograph by Matthew Allen)*

box melodic drone (the great *nāgasvaram* performer T. N. Rajarattinam Pillai is considered in Chapter 4). Muttuttandavar lived near the ancient coastal city of Cidambaram, which was built around a sacred site consecrated to Naṭarāja (Figure 1.8), a local manifestation of Śiva, and has been a major ceremonial center since at least the sixth century A.D. The Naṭarāja temple at Cidambaram is one of the most famous Śiva temples in India. Because of Naṭarāja's legendary association with dance, it is a particularly important pilgrimage site for dancers. Muttuttandavar's chosen personal deity was Naṭarāja, and nearly all of his compositions are dedicated to this deity.

∞

The original "Lord of the Dance." *Naṭarāja literally means king* (rāja) *of dance* (naṭanam). *The legends and mythology associated with Śiva as Naṭarāja are among the most ancient in Hinduism, but the Naṭarāja form of Śiva was not widely known outside South India before the writings of the art historian Ananda Coomaraswamy introduced his iconography and mythology to the non-Hindu world. A South Indian tradition of bronze sculpture dating back to the Cōḻa period (ca. 900–1100 A.D.) portrays Śiva dancing inside an arc of fire. He holds a ḍamaru hourglass-shaped drum and burning embers in one pair of hands. The other pair of hands makes the dance* mudrās, *gestures, for surrendering and protecting. While one leg is uplifted in a dance pose, the other pins down Muyalakan, the dwarf of ignorance, in a posture of submission. Coomaraswamy's essay* Dance of Shiva, *first published in 1918, was a prime factor in generating an avid international interest in these sculptures (Subramaniam 1983; Coomaraswamy 1985), representations of which can be seen in most major art museums today.*

∞

*The Text of "I Trusted You/*Unnai Nambinēn*" (CD track 3).* In a *kriti,* the *pallavi* always serves as an important theme of return, both melodically and textually, because musicians return to it after singing the other sections. In "I Trusted You," the repetitions of the *pallavi* line reinforce the act of devotion the speaker performs—*I trusted you lord, I prostrated myself at your feet.* The composer begins with this thought and ends with it, along the way adding more information about this deity he worships, what renown this Lord has in all the seven worlds. Notice that in the *anupallavi* section he mentions Naṭarāja by name; in *kritis,* the *anupallavi* is usually the place where the composer addresses the god or goddess most directly. It is also in the *anupallavi* that the melody rises to its highest point in a *kriti.*

The description of the iconography and worship of the deity in the *anupallavi* and *caraṇam* sections of "I trusted you" is common in the *kritis* of Muttuttandavar (and developed to an even greater extent in those of Muttusvami Dikshitar). Tyagaraja's *kritis* to Rāma, on the other hand, usually focus less on these types of details than on direct personal expression of his emotional state. The different textual approaches by *kriti* composers illustrate the varieties of *bhakti,* the ways in Hindus express devotion.

ACTIVITY 1.4 *Text and Translation*

Pallavi *(contains one line of text):*

(1) Unnai nambinēn ayyā caraṇam, nān	I trusted you, lord, I prostrated at your feet

Anupallavi *(two lines):*

(1) Punai śambō, nāgam punai śambō naṭarāja	Wearing a cobra, Śiva Naṭarāja . . .
(2) Puliyūr val̲ īśā	Oh Lord who dwells in Cidambaram

Second caraṇam *(four lines):*

(1) Mal̲uviḍai tarikkinr̲a kaiyā konrai	You who hold the embers of fire in your hand
(2) Malar mālai punaihinr̲a vaḍi cuḍar meyyā	You who wear a beautiful flower garland you're fond of, on your body
(3) El̲u buvi tudikkinr̲a tuyyā anbar	You are worshiped throughout the seven continents
(4) Iḍamāy irundu inbam uḍanāḷum ayyā	You reside in the hearts of your devotees with compassion, lord

[Translated from the Tamil̲ by T. Viswanathan]

*The Musical Setting of "I Trusted You/*Unnai Nambinēn*" (CD track 3).* Muttuttandavar composed this *kriti* at least three hundred years ago, but the musical setting with which it is associated today is quite recent, a direct result of the Tamil̲ Music Movement. By the early twentieth century, the melodic settings of many of Muttuttandavar's compositions had been lost, but texts of eighty-five of his songs were available in print, circulating in inexpensive "evening bazaar" editions. Flutist T. N. Swaminatha Pillai was commissioned in 1941 by Annamalai University to compose new musical settings for Muttuttandavar's sixty available *kriti* texts. Swaminatha Pillai was the *guru* of coauthor T. Viswanathan, who heard his teacher compose many of the new musical settings in 1941 and 1942 and learned "I Trusted You" (CD track 3) from him (Figure 1.9).

FIGURE 1.9 *T. N. Swaminatha Pillai, flute, accompanied by T. Viswanathan (seated to his left, in glasses), circa 1948.* *(Courtesy of Jody Cormack Viswanathan)*

∞

Publishing in India. *For many centuries writers in India wrote on dried palm leaves, etching texts onto the leaves using a sharp stylus* (Figures 1.10 and 1.11). *With the coming of mass printing to South India in the mid-nineteenth century, many books of Tamil̲ song texts were brought out in cheap editions that appeared on and almost immediately vanished from streetside* gujili kaḍai *"evening bazaar" bookstalls. A book containing the texts of sixty of Muttuttandavar's Tamil̲* kritis *and twenty-five of his dance* padams *was among these, printed in at least two editions circa 1868 and 1874. These books contained song texts and indications of what* rāga *and* tāḷa *(melodic mode and rhythmic cycle, respectively; see Chapter 2) the songs were to be performed in, but no notation of melodies. When the Tamil̲ Music Movement started, these*

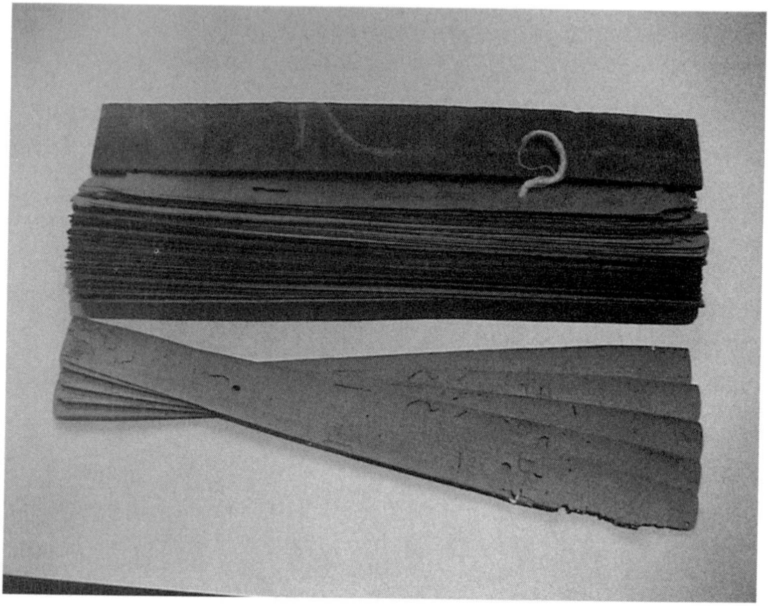

FIGURE 1.10 *Palm leaf manuscript with binding boards. T. Viswanathan collection. (Photograph by Matthew Allen)*

> *editions were the primary written sources available, and many of the Annamalai University editions of the 1940s onward, incorporating solfège-based musical notation, were based on them.*

∞

The Group's Progress Through the Kriti. The path musicians take through a *kriti* is more complicated than the path through a *bhajan*, and, very importantly, it is somewhat flexible. There are widely followed conventions—for example, more often than not a line of text is repeated before the next line is sung—but performance gives options to the musicians at each step of the way. The musicians are not following a written score; they work their way through the composition line by line, in the moment. The Karṇāṭak group has a leader (in this case the vocalist) who is not constrained by having several other people simultaneously singing the piece, so it is relatively easy for him or her to mold the form

FIGURE 1.11 *Palm leaf (detail). T. Viswanathan collection.* (*Photograph by Matthew Allen*)

of the *kriti* in performance. If the leader feels like repeating a line one, two, or three times before moving to the next line, she or he simply does it, and the accompanists follow, listening closely, ready to move to the next line when the leader does. The similarity in size and intimacy of a Karṇāṭak group to both a string quartet and a small jazz combo are apparent here. In the way Karṇāṭak musicians proceed through a *kriti* by ear rather than by following a written score, the comparison to a small jazz combo becomes even more compelling. While you follow along with the listening guide in Activity 1.5 listen in particular for evidence of how the violin and double-headed membranophone *mridaṅgam* interact with and follow the vocalist.

Listen to the *kriti* (CD track 3) while following the listening guide (Activity 1.5). Describe the interaction between the musicians, noting elements of this performance that strike you as similar to or different from the *bhajan* example. Try to identify points at which the vocalist T. Viswanathan introduces subtle melodic variations when he repeats a line of text, and describe what relationship you think the audible clapping may have to the rhythmic organization of the music (tāḷa will be discussed in Chapter 2). The lines of each section of the *kriti* are labeled numerically to facilitate reference to the listening guide. Of the three *caraṇams* for this song, Viswanathan sings only the second.

ACTIVITY 1.5 *Listening Guide for* Kriti *"I Trusted You/*Unnai Nambinēn*" (CD track 3). Rāga: Kīravāṇi; Tāḷa:* ādi *(eight-beat cycle); T. Viswanathan, vocalist; Anantha Krishnan, violin; David Nelson,* mridaṅgam

Time	Tāḷa cycle	Section and line	Text and performance notes
		Pallavi	
0:01	1	1	*Unnai nambinēn ayyā caraṇam, nān*
0:08	2	1	*Unnai nambinēn ayyā caraṇam, nān*
0:14	3	1	*Unnai nambinēn ayyā caraṇam, nān* —melodic variation on the word *unnai*
0:20	4	1	*Unnai nambinēn ayyā caraṇam, nān*
0:26	5	1	*Unnai nambinēn ayyā*
0:32	6	1	Vocalist sustains syllable ā
		Anupallavi	
0:39	7	1	*Punai śambō, nāgam* —Vocalist sustains syllable *bō* before continuing to *nāgam*
0:45	8	1	*Punai śambō naṭarāja*
0:51	9	1	*Punai śambō naṭarāja*
0:57	10	2	*Puliyūr vaḻīśā*
1:03	11	1	*Punai śambō naṭarāja*
1:09	12	2	*Puliyūr vaḻīśā*
		Pallavi reprise	
1:15	13	1	*Unnai nambi* . . . (coughing) . . . *caraṇam, nān*
1:20	14	1	*Unnai nambi* . . . (coughing)
1:26	15		Vocalist sustains syllable *ā*

		Caraṇam	
1:32	16	1	*Maluviḍai tarikkinra kaiyā, konrai*
1:38	17	2	*Malar mālai punaihinra vaḍi cuḍar meyyā*
1:44	18	1	*Maluviḍai tarikkinra kaiyā, konrai*
1:49	19	2	*Malar mālai punaihinra vaḍi cuḍar meyyā*
1:55	20	3	*Elu buvi tudikkinra*
			Vocalist sustains syllable *ā*
2:01	21	3	*Elu buvi tudikkinra tuyyā anbar*
2:07	22	4	*Iḍamāy irundu inbam uḍanāḷum ayyā*
2:13	23	3	*Elu buvi tudikkinra tuyyā anbar*
2:18	24	4	*Iḍamāy irundu inbam uḍanāḷum ayyā*
		Pallavi reprise	
2:24	25	1	*Unnai nambinēn ayyā caraṇam, nān*
2:30	26	1	*Unnai nambinēn ayyā*
2:35	27		Vocalist sustains syllable *ā*
2:41			[Ends]

The Ensemble. In most Karṇāṭak concerts the performing ensemble is smaller than a typical *bhajan* group. It includes the soloist (vocalist or instrumentalist) who sits in the center of the stage, flanked by a melodic accompanist, usually a violinist, and a rhythmic accompanist, most often a player of the double-headed *mridaṅgam* (see Figure 1.13). A fourth person, often a student of the main artist, plays a supporting chordophone called *tambūra*, which provides an essential function called *śruti*, a steady melodic drone background. If the soloist is a vocalist, the *tambūra* player is often the soloist's student and sings a supporting vocal part. There is sometimes a second percussionist, who may play either the small lizardskin frame drum *kañjīra* (heard on CD track 1), similar to a tambourine; the *ghaṭam*, an open-top tuned clay pot idiophone; or the *morsing*, a jaw harp idiophone.

The Instruments

Violin (chordophone). Like the harmonium, the European violin (Figure 1.12) was introduced into India approximately two centuries ago, but while harmonium came in the train of Christian missionaries, the

FIGURE 1.12 *V. Tyagarajan, Karṇāṭak violinist.* *(Courtesy of Jody Cormack Viswanathan)*

violin was introduced in a secular capacity. It formed part of the Tañjāvūr palace band assembled by Rāja Serfoji II (ruled 1798–1832); the palace records show the name of an English violinist, Jon Sylvester, on the payroll during Serfoji's reign. Because the violin has no frets, the player's fingers can slide freely all along the strings, making it a very expressive instrument capable of articulating the melodic subtleties of Indian music. Today violin accompanies almost every Karṇāṭak concert and is a popular solo instrument as well. While the harmonium was eventually rejected in Karṇāṭak music circles—condemned as a Western abomination—the equally Western but more flexible violin was embraced:

> There was something about the violin—its Westernness and newness but also its uncanny ability to imitate the Karṇāṭak voice—that made

> it quintessentially modern, flexible and resilient enough to withstand various experiments. Like recording technology, the violin provided a way of reproducing the voice, a new way of representing Karṇāṭak music. (Weidman 2001:64)

Mridaṅgam *(Membranophone).* The *mridaṅgam* (Figure 1.13) is the ubiquitous membranophone of South India, the primary percussion instrument in most all Karṇāṭak concerts. Its low, woody, earthy tone—quite a contrast to the brilliant crisp sounds of the North Indian *tablā* and *bāyā* pair—is a fixture on the Karṇāṭak soundscape. It is made from a hollowed-out piece of jackwood about sixty centimeters long. The heads are constructed of several layers of goat, cow, and water buffalo hide. The right head contains a semipermanent round black spot in its center, made of a mix of boiled white rice and powdered black *kiṭṭān* stone. This spot enables it to be tuned precisely to the tonic pitch of the main artist. The left head is not precisely tuned; a ball of *rava* wheat flour or farina (some players today use silicone caulk instead) is applied

FIGURE 1.13 *Brothers T. Ranganathan,* mridaṅgam, *and T. Viswanathan, flute.* *(Courtesy of Jan Steward)*

to this head at the beginning of a performance; this helps it articulate a low booming sound, the pitch of which is changed by pressure applied to the head. The *mridaṅgam* can articulate no fewer than fifteen distinct sounds, all of which have names in a system of mnemonic syllables (see Chapter 2). Listeners whose ears are accustomed to full drum sets with complements of tom toms, cymbals, and other coloristic percussion instruments may initially find the *mridaṅgam* sound rather sparse and spartan. Once one's ears begin to get used to the *mridaṅgam*, however, its wide spectrum of tonal colors and voices becomes apparent.

Tambūra *(Chordophone) and Its* Śruti, *Drone, Function.* The South Indian *tambūra* is an elegant long-necked lute, usually made of very thin jackwood (see Figure 4.2, photograph of T. Brinda seated with *tambūra*). Its neck and round bowl are hollow and the instrument weighs only a few pounds. It voices a recurring melodic pattern that reinforces the tonal center throughout a concert. Activity 1.6 takes the note C as the tonic pitch for purposes of illustration; in practice musicians choose whatever tonic pitch best suits them. The distinctive buzzing sound of the *tambūra* is created by placing a small piece of string under each playing wire at a precise nodal point along the curved bridge, which brings out the overtones or partials above the fundamental note (Reck, in Arnold 2000:356). In addition to *tambūra* other instruments are sometimes used to provide the drone, including the *śruti peṭṭi* drone box, a bellows-operated aerophone, and electronic digitally sampled tone generators.

ACTIVITY 1.6. *Try creating your own drone by sounding the notes indicated below on the piano while holding down the sustain pedal or by open tuning a guitar to sound notes in a dominant-tonic relationship, allowing each note to ring as long as possible without muting. If circumstances permit, invent ways to "prepare" your piano or guitar to produce slight buzzes when the strings are set in motion. Choose a G near the middle of your instrument's range, followed by the C above it (played twice) and then the C below it.*

Notes of tambūra drone:

middle G–high C–high C–low C

SUMMARY

In this chapter, two types of song were introduced and compared. Their musical structure and performance contexts were discussed and compared, together with the musical instruments and ensembles involved. Activities have been structured to encourage critical listening and participatory engagement with the audio selections. The chapter has discussed the importance of composers in South India and has begun to introduce the religious, linguistic, and sociopolitical contexts in which the music lives in South India, a discussion that will be developed through the course of the book.

CHAPTER 2

Key Concepts in Karṇāṭak Music

This chapter introduces important concepts that underpin Karṇāṭak music, giving musicians a basis upon which to express themselves and listeners a basis on which to appreciate what they hear. The discussion focuses on *rāga* and *tāḷa,* the melodic and rhythmic parameters within which Karṇāṭak music occurs. Almost every composition in Karṇāṭak music is set in a rāga and a tāḷa. During the course of a performance of a piece, these parameters do not change; once musicians begin a composition, they stay in the same rāga and tāḷa throughout, excepting the very occasional *rāgamālikā* or *tāḷamālikā,* "garland" of rāgas or tāḷas.

The reader familiar with European or American music will note that the word harmony does not come into play here. The Karṇāṭak and Hindustāni music systems do not use functional harmony, a fundamental principle of most European and American music. In Karṇāṭak music there is no concept of a chord (triad) and, therefore, no concept of chord changes. While there is a concept of tonal center (the Karṇāṭak solfège syllable *sa* is the equivalent of the European *do*), there is no concept of key or of modulation between keys. In Karṇāṭak music subtleties of melody and rhythm reign supreme.

TĀḶA: METER AND RHYTHM IN KARṆĀṬAK MUSIC

Tenṟal vaḍivum śivanār tiruvaḍivum
If one can see the form of the Southern breeze, the holy form of Śiva,
Anṟal vaḍivum madan vaḍivum
The form of scent, the form of Madan (Cupid),
Kunṟāda vēyin iśai vaḍivum vēda vaḍivum
The form of the flute tone, the form of the Vēdas,
Kaṇil lāya tāḷam kāṇalām
One can see the subtlety of the tāḷa

Tunga Munivar (quoted in Sambamurthy 1968:18)

A Karṇāṭak composition is set to a metrical cycle called tāḷa. Each tāḷa contains a number of *akṣarās*, individual beats or counts, grouped into larger units called *aṅgas*, literally, "limbs." In Karṇāṭak (although not Hindustāni) music the tempo at which the tāḷa moves stays constant throughout a piece, so that at least in theory, there is no speeding up or slowing down of the basic beats of the tāḷa. The fact that the metrical structure and tempo of a piece do not change might appear to impose restraints on rhythmic creativity, but as will be shown, a Karṇāṭak drummer has many options available to generate rhythmic interest besides changes of meter or tempo.

The Five "Families" of Rhythm and Drummers' Thinking. In Karṇāṭak rhythmic thinking, five numbers have primary importance. The numbers 4, 3, 7, 5, and 9 constitute the five *jātis*—varieties, classes, or families of Karṇāṭak rhythm (as explained in Chapter 1, *jāti* is also the term for hereditary social grouping, caste). They are traditionally listed in this order because the numbers 4 and 3 were the first to be recognized by theorists as a legitimate basis on which to build a tāḷa; over time, the others were gradually incorporated. These five numbers—4, 3, 7, 5, and 9—permeate Karṇāṭak rhythmic thinking, both at a macro level as building blocks out of which lengthy improvisations are structured and at a micro level as the five ways in which an individual beat may be internally subdivided—into fourths, thirds, sevenths, fifths, or ninths (in the activities that follow individual beats are subdivided into four pulses).

Practice saying the following syllable sequences—called *solkaṭṭu*, "bundles of syllables"—for the five *jātis* of Karṇāṭak rhythm (Activity 2.1). A dot under a consonant indicates that it is retroflex; to achieve this sound, roll your tongue back, placing the tip against the roof of your mouth, then as you voice the consonant flip your tongue forward and down. The dashes in the middle of the longer *jātis* have no time value; they indicate only how a *jāti* is conceptually subdivided.

ACTIVITY 2.1 Solkaṭṭu *Syllables for the Five* Jātis *of Karṇāṭak Rhythm*

4	*Caturaśra "four-sided"*	*ta ka di mi (or) ta ka jo ṇu (or) ta ka di na*
3	*Tiśra "three-sided"*	*ta ki ṭa*

7	*Miśra "mixed"*	*ta ki ṭa - ta ka di mi*
5	*Khaṇḍa "broken"*	*ta ka - ta ki ṭa*
9	*Saṅkīrṇa "all mixed up"*	*ta ka di mi - ta ka - ta ki ṭa*

Hand Gestures and Vocalized Syllable Sequences for Commonly Used Tāḷas. Musicians and audience members indicate progress through tāḷa visually and audibly by using *kriyā,* hand gestures. These include clapping with palm down (abbreviated in Activity 2.2 as [C]) or upturned [Cu]; turning the palm up in a hand wave [W]; and finger counts, touching the fingers of one hand [pinky, ring, etc.] to the palm of the other hand or the thigh.

South Indian musicians have evolved *solkaṭṭu* in order to voice rhythmic groupings quickly and efficiently. *Solkaṭṭu* sequences such as those in Activity 2.1 are constructed to require minimal changes in mouth position, unlike the English numerals *one, two, three* or their Tamiḻ equivalents *onṟu, irendu,* and *mūnṟu,* which were not designed with speed of recitation in mind. As a result, *solkaṭṭu* is well matched to the challenges of counting and combining the *jātis,* sometimes at very high rates of speed.

Rhythmic syllables and drumming. *In Karṇāṭak music there is a close link between the* solkaṭṭu *rhythmic syllables and actual drumming. Right from the beginning lessons, drumming students are taught rhythmic patterns from two perspectives: They learn to play patterns directly on the* mridaṅgam *and to recite these patterns in* solkaṭṭu. *Every drum stroke has a corresponding syllable, and the student learns the two together.*

In Activity 2.2, appropriate hand gestures and *solkaṭṭu* sequences of vocal syllables are given for several popular tāḷas. The next several activities are designed either for two students or two groups of students. One person or group should clap the hand gestures associated with the tāḷa while the other vocally recites its *solkaṭṭu.* After some time practicing, switch roles so that each person experiences both activities. Then, once everyone is comfortable doing both separately, try clapping the tāḷa and reciting its *solkaṭṭu* at the same time.

A few notes may help in doing this activity: When a limb contains more beats than there are fingers on the hand, as in the seven-beat limb of *miśra jhampa* tāḷa, the counting continues onto the thumb and then starts back around on the pinky again. Also, the last two tāḷas in the list, *miśra cāpu* and *khaṇḍa cāpu*, believed to have originated from folk practice, are counted quickly and energetically.

ACTIVITY 2.2 *Common Karṇāṭak Tāḷas, with Hand Gestures and Spoken* Solkaṭṭu *Sequences*

Key to hand gestures: C, clap with palm down; Cu, clap with palm up; W, wave; "pinky," etc., finger counts

1. Ādi *(eight-beat cycle, grouped into three aṅgas, 4 + 2 + 2 beats)*

(beats)
1 . . . 2 . . . 3 . . . 4 . . . 5 . . . 6 . . . 7 . . . 8 . . .

(gestures)

C	pinky	ring	middle	C	W	C	W

(*solkaṭṭu*)

ta	ka	di	mi	ta	ka	jo	ṇu

2. Rūpaka *(three-beat cycle)*

1 . . . 2 . . . 3 . . .

C	C	W
ta	ki	ṭa

3. Tiśra ēka *(another name for, and way to count, a three-beat cycle)*

1 . . . 2 . . . 3

C	pinky	ring
ta	ki	ṭa

4. Miśra Jhampa *(ten-beat cycle, grouped 7 + 1 + 2)*

1 . . .	2 . . .	3 . . .	4 . . .	5 . . .	6 . . .	7 . . .	8 . . .	9 . . .	10 . . .
C	pinky	ring	middle	index	thumb	pinky	C	C	W
ta	ki	ṭa	ta	ka	di	mi	ta	ta	ka

5. Tiśra Tripuṭa *(relatively slow seven-beat cycle, grouped 3 + 2 + 2)*

1 . . .	2 . . .	3 . . .	4 . . .	5 . . .	6 . . .	7 . . .
C	pinky	ring	C	W	C	W
ta	ki	ṭa	ta	ka	di	mi

6. Miśra Cāpu *(relatively fast seven-beat cycle, grouped 3 + 2 + 2)*

1 . . .	2 . . .	3 . . .	4 . . .	5 . . .	6 . . .	7 . . .
Cu	Cu		C		C	
ta	ki	ṭa	ta	ka	di	mi

7. Khaṇḍa Cāpu *(fast five-beat cycle, grouped 2 + 3)*

1 . . .	2 . . .	3 . . .	4 . . .	5 . . .
C		C	C	
ta	ka	ta	ki	ṭa

Tāḷa Exercises in Three Speeds. One way that rhythmic interest is generated is by doubling and redoubling the speed of vocal recitation while maintaining the constant rate of progress through the tāḷa with hand gestures. Doubling and redoubling against an unchanging pulse is a fundamental procedure that Karṇāṭak students undergo in all training exercises, whether melodic or rhythmic. Doubling the recitation is called "second speed," and redoubling is called "third speed." Activity 2.3 illustrates this procedure in *ādi* tāḷa, using the sequences *ta ka di mi* and *ta ka jo ṇu* as the basis for recitation. First, listen to CD track 4 while following the notation (each line is recited twice on the CD throughout these rhythmic activities, as is customary for this type of exercise). Then do the activity with a partner or split the class into two groups of students, one keeping the tāḷa while the other recites, reversing roles periodically. Finally, when you are comfortable with each separately, do the recitation while keeping the tāḷa.

ACTIVITY 2.3 *Exercise in* Ādi Tāḷa, Solkaṭṭu *Recitation in Three Speeds (CD Track 4)*

[beats]
1 . . . 2 . . . 3 . . . 4 . . . 5 . . . 6 . . . 7 . . . 8 . . .

[gestures]
C pinky ring middle C W C W

[first speed]
ta ka di mi ta ka jo ṇu

[second speed]
ta ka di mi ta ka jo ṇu ta ka di mi ta ka jo ṇu

[third speed]
t k d m t k j ṇ t k d m t k j ṇ t k d m t k j ṇ t k d m t k j ṇ

Note: Each line of the solkaṭṭu *is recited twice; at third speed, only the first letter of each syllable is given for reasons of space.*

Reciting *solkaṭṭu* for *ādi* tāḷa is relatively simple at doublings of speed because the structure of the tāḷa is duple; the doubled and redoubled recitation continues to basically coincide with the hand gestures. Taking the same exercise in a tāḷa cycle containing an odd instead of even number of beats presents new challenges. Activity 2.4 shows the same three-speed exercise, now set in the seven-beat *tiśra tripuṭa* tāḷa, using the sequence *ta ki ṭa - ta ka di mi* as the basis for recitation. Follow the same procedure as for the previous activities. Notice that when reciting at second speed, after finishing the seven-pulse pattern the first time, the first pulse (*ta*) of the next pattern falls *between* beats four and five, not on a beat. This may be a disorienting experience at first, but with practice it will begin to make sense!

ACTIVITY 2.4 *Exercise in* Tiśra Tripuṭa Tāḷa, Solkaṭṭu *Recitation in Three Speeds (CD Track 5)*

[beats]
1 . . . 2 . . . 3 . . . 4 . . . 5 . . . 6 . . . 7 . . .

[gestures]
C pinky ring C W C W

[first speed]
ta ki ṭa ta ka di mi

[second speed]
ta ki ṭa ta ka di mi- ta ki ṭa ta ka di mi

[third speed]
t k ṭ t k d m-t k ṭ t k d m-t k ṭ t k d m-t k ṭ t k d m

Note: Each line of solkattu is recited twice; dashes inserted at second and third speeds show where the seven-pulse pattern finishes.

A different type of exercise (Activity 2.5) set in the three-beat *tiśra ēka* tāḷa involves introducing successive changes to a set of rhythmic syllables. After first reciting the three-syllable phrase *ta ki ṭa* in three speeds (numbered as 1), *ta* and *ka* are combined with a rest (,) in three permutations (numbers 2–4). As with the previous activities, work with a partner or in two groups until you are able to do the recitation while keeping the tāḷa.

ACTIVITY 2.5 *Exercise in* Tiśra Ēka Tāḷa, Solkaṭṭu *Recitation in Three Speeds (CD Track 6)*

Beats: 1 . . . 2 . . . 3 . . .
Hand gestures: C pinky ring

(1; begins at 0:11)
First speed: ta ki ṭa
Second speed: ta ki ṭa - ta ki ṭa
Third speed: ta ki ṭa- ta ki ṭa-ta ki ṭa- ta ki ṭa

(2; begins at 0:32)	1	.	.	.	2	.	.	.	3	.	.	.
First speed:	ta				ka				,			
Second speed:	ta		ka		,		- ta		ka		,	
Third speed:	ta	ka	,-	ta	ka	,-	ta	ka	,-	ta	ka	,
(3; begins at 0:50)												
First speed:	ta				,				ka			
Second speed:	ta		,		ka		-ta		,		ka	
Third speed:	ta	,	ka-ta		,	ka-ta		,	ka-	ta	,	ka
(4; begins at 1:05)												
First speed:	,				ta				ka			
Second speed:	,		ta		ka		-,		ta		ka	
Third speed:	,	ta	ka-,		ta	ka-,		ta	ka- ,		ta	ka

Note: each line of solkaṭṭu *is recited twice; dashes inserted at second and third speeds show where the three-pulse pattern finishes.*

The three-pulse rhythmic phrases presented in Activity 2.5 can be combined within a single cycle of tāḷa to create more diverse phrases. Activity 2.6, in third speed only, is one way *mridaṅgam* performer David Nelson shows students the large number of possible combinations that can be made out of groupings of three.

ACTIVITY 2.6 *Exercise Combining Phrases in* Tiśra Ēka Tāḷa, *Third Speed (CD Track 7)*

Beats:	1 . . . 2 . . . 3 . . .
Hand gestures:	C pinky ring
Third speed:	ta ki ṭa-ta , ka-ta ki ṭa-ta , ka
	ta , ka-ta ki ṭa-ta , ka-ta ki ṭa
	ta ka , -ta , ka-ta ka , -ta , ka
	ta , ka-ta ka , -ta , ka-ta ka ,

Note: Each line of solkaṭṭu *is recited twice.*

RĀGA: MELODY IN KARṆĀṬAK MUSIC

In the opinion of the wise, that particularity of notes and melodic movements, or that distinction of melodic sound by which one is delighted, is rāga.

—*Matanga's* Bṛhaddēśi, *circa 800* A.D. *(quoted in Widdess 1995:41)*

Over a millennium ago, Matanga was the first in a long line of erudite scholars to write on rāga. Like tāḷa, rāga is a vast topic, central to the understanding of Indian music. What is rāga? Like a Euro-American scale, a rāga can be summarized as a collection of notes or pitches. And musicians recognize particular melodies or tunes as belonging to a rāga. But scale or tune can only begin to give a notion of rāga. To the Indian musician or listener a rāga is more. It is at once a storehouse of remembered melodic history and a body of melodic potential to be drawn upon and realized in performance, a bit like a box of painters' colors. Indeed, the word rāga comes from the verbal root *rañj,* to be colored a reddish tint. Rāga has colored the minds of millions of listeners over the centuries. While the study of rāga has many complexities, it is important to remember that as with tāḷa, rāga is *not* just a technical subject. Its root idea comes from and returns to the giving of pleasure, to painting with sounds, to coloring the mind. There are hundreds of living rāgas and thousands of potential ones, although in concert practice today about fifty to one hundred rāgas are heard on a regular basis. The present discussion of rāga focuses on Indian concepts usually—although imperfectly—represented in English as *scale, note, ornamentation, phrase,* and *functional note.*

Scale. Contemporary Karṇāṭak musicians use the concept of scale as a kind of shorthand for rāgas, a way to briefly summarize their melodic shape and content. The word scale comes from *scala,* the Latin term for ladder. A musical scale can be thought of as a ladder of notes, a series of musical steps leading from a fundamental or tonic to its octave. A Karṇāṭak rāga must have between five and seven constituent melodic steps called *svaras* (literally, "radiating selves"), the closest available South Indian cognate to the European concept of the note or tone. Rāgas are conceived of as having both ascending and descending directions (*ārōhaṇa* and *avarōhaṇa*, respectively), which may or may not contain the same *svaras.* A raga may contain all seven steps in both its ascending and descending directions and may move strictly in a stepwise fashion both up and down. But there are other possibilities—a rāga may be pentatonic or hexatonic, and one or more scalar steps may be skipped in one or both directions. And, while some rāgas move straight up and down in stepwise scalar fashion, others do not: Some of the most beautiful rāgas are *vakra*, crooked, starting to move in one direction then temporarily reversing direction before continuing in the original direction.

The classification of South Indian rāgas by scale type is a relatively recent development, having been first proposed about four hundred years ago and gradually becoming more and more widespread. Today, an ingenious symmetrical scheme of seventy-two scales first proposed by the theorist Venkatamakhi around 1620, called the *mēḷakartā* system, is used to classify all South Indian rāgas (Pesch 1999:103–105). For many centuries, however, rāgas were primarily grouped by nonmusical considerations such as seasons, time of day, or familial relations. Some rāgas were associated with the coming of the monsoon, others with rocking babies to sleep or curing illnesses. Some were grouped into familial schemes including mother, father, and children. In ancient South India, a highly articulated system of musical modes, the Tamiḻ *paṇ*, associated particular melodies with the five landscapes of the region. Rāgas have also been affiliated with particular times of day or night, outside of which it was considered inauspicious to perform them. This custom is still widely observed in North India, where, for example, a morning or evening rāga is not often performed outside of its intended time of day. While this practice has largely died out in Karṇāṭak concerts, it remains a strong consideration in the music of temple *nāgasvaram* traditions (see Chapter 4) and in associations of particular rāgas with particular effects, such as the persistent use of the rāga Nīlāmbari as a lullaby.

Note (Svara) *and Solfège Syllable Names.* Each of the seven *svaras* has a solfège name, somewhat analogous to the system of syllables used in European music. The Karṇāṭak solfège syllables not only serve pedagogical functions similar to European solfege but also become the basis for improvisation in performance (see discussion of *svara kalpana* in Chapter 3). Unlike in European solfège, each of the seven Karṇāṭak *svara* names is used to refer to the flat, natural, or sharped values of a particular *svara* (for example, the same term *ri* is used to refer to the second degree of the rāga, whether it is a minor, major, or augmented second). The European solfège syllables and their South Indian counterparts are shown together in Activity 2.7. Practice reciting the *svaras* in both ascending and descending directions, as a prelude to Activities 2.13 and 2.14.

ACTIVITY 2.7 *Corresponding Names for European and Karṇāṭak Melodic Solfège Syllables, Ascending in Pitch from Left to Right*

sa	ri	ga	ma	pa	dha	ni	s̄a
do	re	mi	fa	sol	la	ti	do

Kīravāṇi and Kāpi Rāgas: Rāga as a "Vast Ocean". We will now examine two rāgas in greater detail, Kīravāṇi and Kāpi. Two examples of each of these rāgas are included on the compact disc: the *kriti* presented on CD track 3 and the extended performance built around a *kriti* in CD tracks 13–17 are both set in Kīravāṇi, while the *bhajan* (CD track 1) and a composition called *jāvaḷi* (CD track 18) are in Kāpi. Using *svara* syllables and European note names, basic scalar summaries of these two rāgas are given in Activities 2.8 and 2.9 (CD track 8 and CD track 9).

In Activity 2.8a, try to match the pitch of the singer, using the solfège names to sing the unornamented Kīravāṇi scale (CD track 8, 0:00–0:38). Then while listening to the scale with its traditional ornamentation in Activity 2.8b (CD track 8, 0:39-1:04) write down which *svaras* you hear as ornamented, and which as plain (the detailed descriptive notation in Activity 2.8b will help you in this respect).

∞

Detailed descriptive notation. *Over the course of teaching Karṇāṭak music in the United States for four decades, coauthor T. Viswanathan developed a system of* svara *notation recording fine details of melodic ornamentation to meet the needs of his non-Indian students. This system involves melodic notation at two levels: A bottom level (with the* svara *names spelled out in full, e.g.,* sa, ri, *etc.) represents basic conceptual* svaras, *while an upper level (abbreviated as* s, r, *etc.) describes the actual detailed pitches used in the ornamentation of particular* svaras.

For example, in Activity 2.8b, the first detailed ornament in the ascending direction occurs on ga. *Taking C as the* sa, *tonal center, for the sake of convenience, the pitch details of the ornamentation are* ma ri ma ri ma ri ma ri (*written as* m r m r m r m r), *corresponding to the pitches F D F D F D F D.*

ACTIVITY 2.8A *Kīravāṇi Rāga Scale Without Ornamentation (CD Track 8, 0:00–0:38)*

Ārōhaṇa *(ascent)*

sa	ri	ga	ma	pa	dha	ni	s̄a
C	D	E♭	F	G	A♭	B	c

Avarōhaṇa *(descent)*

s̄a	ni	dha	pa	ma	ga	ri	sa
c	B	A♭	G	F	E♭	D	C

Note: The pitch C is taken as tonal center for reasons of convenience.

ACTIVITY 2.8B *Kīravāṇi Rāga Scale with Its Traditional Ornamentation, Using Detailed Descriptive Notation (CD Track 8, 0:39–1:04)*

Ārōhaṇa *(ascent)*

```
s , , , r , , , mrmrmrmr m , , , p , , , dpdpd, , ndsnsnsn s , , ,
sa, , , ri, , , ga, , ,  ma, , , pa, , , dha, , , ni, , ,  s̄a, , ,
```

Avarōhaṇa *(descent)*

```
p/s , , snsnsnsn dpdpdpdp dmp , , m , , , mrmrmrmg r , , , s , , ,
s̄a, , , ni, , ,  dha, , , pa, , , ma, , , ga, , ,   ri, , , sa, , ,
```

Note: In the upper level of the descriptive notation, only the first letter of each svara *is used, for reasons of space and to distinguish it from the lower, conceptual level; commas generally indicate a held note rather than a rest.*

In Activity 2.9 follow the same procedure as in the previous activity. Make note of as many ways as you can in which the two rāgas differ.

ACTIVITY 2.9A *Kāpi Rāga Scale Without Ornamentation (CD Track 9, 0:00–0:32)*

Ārōhaṇa *(ascent)*

sa	ri	ma	pa	ni	s̄a
C	D	F	G	B	c

Avarōhaṇa *(descent)*

s̄a	ni	dha	ni	pa	ma	ga	ri	sa
c	B♭	A	B♭	G	F	E♭	D	C

ACTIVITY 2.9B *Kāpi Rāga Scale with Its Traditional Ornamentation, Using Detailed Descriptive Notation (CD Track 9,0:37–0:54)*

Ārōhaṇa *(ascent)*

s , , , $\overline{\text{mrmrmr}}$, m , , , p , , , $\overline{\text{snsns}}$, s , , ,
sa, , , ri, , , ma, , , pa, , , ni, , , s̄a , , ,

Avarōhaṇa *(descent)*

s d s , n d n , d , , , $\overline{\text{sndn}}$, , p , , , m , , , g r g , r , , , s , , ,
$\overline{\text{sa}}$, , , ni, , , dha, , , ni, , , pa, , , ma, , , ga, , , ri, , , sa, , ,

Just two such scalar summaries can begin to suggest the variety of possibilities within rāga. Kīravāṇi contains the same seven *svaras* in ascent and descent, going straight up and down the scale without any *vakra* crooked motion. Its basic pitches correspond to the European harmonic minor scale, including (relative to the major scale) flatted *ga* and *dha,* third and sixth degrees. The basic scalar summary of Kāpi is very different. In its ascent it is pentatonic, while in the descent it includes all seven *svaras. Ni,* the seventh degree of the scale, is natural in the ascent but flattened in the descent. And the scale includes a *vakra,* crooked, phrase in the first half of the descent, going down *s̄a ni dha,* then returning back up to *ni* before continuing downward.

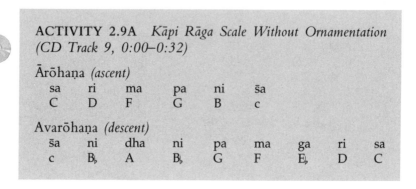

Rāgas North and South. *Kīravāṇi and Kāpi rāgas illuminate a history of border crossings between rāgas in North and South India. Kīravāṇi, a relatively young South Indian rāga that became known through the compositions of the composer Tyagaraja, has in the last several decades become popular in North India, where, as Kirvāni, it is considered a night rāga. Kāpi rāga as practiced today in the South is often called Hindustāni Kāpi because of its similarities to North Indian practice. The Experts Committee of the Music Academy of Madras (today Chennai) declared with some alarm in 1933 that Kāpi rāga had taken on so many features of North Indian music that it had displaced the traditional Karṇāṭak Kāpi, recommending that prescriptive measures be taken to keep it from "straying further" and designating the rāga as popularly practiced "Hindustāni Kāpi."*

Ornamentation (Gamaka). In European musical practice the basic unit, the note or tone, is understood as a fixed pitch. Striking a note on the piano produces an acoustic vibration of a steady, measurable, frequency. *Svaras* sometimes sound like European notes, but as is clear from CD track 8 and CD track 9, they often sound fundamentally different. This is partly because of the integral role of ornamentation (*gamaka*, literally, graces or gracefulness) as a part of *svara*. The ornament in Karṇāṭak music is not considered an add-on to the basic note; *gamaka* is an integral structural part of *svara*. There are many different types of ornamentation in Karṇāṭak music, grouped into three general categories: *kampita* shakes or oscillations, *jāru* slides, and *jaṇṭa* stresses (Activity 2.10, CD track 10). While vibrato is on the palette of ornaments used in Karṇāṭak music, it is one among many possibilities, not a basic part of vocal production as in *bel canto* European vocal training.

In any given rāga, some *svaras* are rendered plain without ornamentation while others "take" particular *gamakas*. Ornamentation varies from rāga to rāga; that is, a *svara* may be ornamented one way in one rāga and another way in a different rāga. A student learns how to appropriately ornament particular *svaras* in particular rāgas through listening and imitating, ideally through a substantial period of apprenticeship with a *guru,* teacher and guide. In Activity 2.10, try imitating the details of ornamentation while listening to CD track 10.

ACTIVITY 2.10 *Three Major Categories of* Gamaka, *Illustrated in Kīravāṇi Rāga (CD Track 10)*

Kampita, *shake (0:00–0:28)*
GA - sa ri GA - <u>ma</u> <u>pa</u> <u>dha</u> <u>NI</u>
Jāru, *slide (0:30–0:48)*
/<u>PA</u> <u>ma</u> - /<u>DHA</u> <u>pa</u> - /<u>NI\dha</u> - /SA <u>ni</u> - /SA - \<u>PA</u> - \<u>SA</u>
Jaṇṭa, *stress (0:50–1:07)*
GA ri - sa SA ri GA ri - sa SA ri RI ga GA ma MA pa PA

Note: Svaras *taking the designated ornament are capitalized; dashes indicate a pause by the singer; "/" and "\" indicate upward and downward slides, respectively; a line under a* svara *indicates it is in the lower octave.*

Phrase **(Sañcāra** *or* **Prayōga).** Musical phrases, groupings of two or more *svaras* called *sañcāra* or *prayōga,* are extremely important components of rāga. Each rāga contains its characteristic phrases, just as *svaras* have appropriate ornamentation. Phrases are prime carriers of the *bhava,* the feeling of a rāga; listeners often speak of how they remember hearing treasured rāga phrases performed by legendary stalwarts of the past. Characteristic phrases also uniquely identify a rāga. Karṇāṭak musicians do not often announce in advance what rāgas or compositions they will perform, nor are concert program notes usually distributed to the audience. When a musician begins to sing or play a rāga, very often she or he begins by rendering one of its characteristic phrases. *Rasikas,* knowledgeable listeners in the audience, will immediately identify the rāga on the basis of this one phrase. There is no need for the musician to sing or play all the way up and down the scale for the *rasika* to be able to identify the rāga.

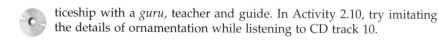

The extent to which phrases are integral to particular rāgas is a complex question. There is evidence that as the scalar view of rāga has slowly become more and more influential in South India, phrase has been deemphasized. In some central ways, an emphasis on scale—a movement straight up and down—works at cross-purposes to an emphasis on phrase. The beauty of phrases lies in the way they bring out the expressive power of a particular region of a rāga, and this often involves some kind of *vakra*, crooked, motion. In rāgas recognized as older, phrases are usually extremely important, while newer rāgas—like those in which Tyagaraja adventurously composed *kritis* for the first time, such as Kīravāṇi—tend to be more scalar in orientation, with fewer characteristic phrases.

Phrases in Kīravāṇi and Kāpi Rāgas. Activity 2.11 (CD track 11) was recorded by co-author Viswanathan to highlight some of the important Kīravāṇi rāga phrases T. Brinda sings in her extended *ālāpana* melodic improvisation (CD track 13, discussed in Chapter 3). We have divided the phrases into two groups. The first, "characteristic" phrases, are primarily stepwise and scalar. The second group, which we have chosen to call "special" phrases, is marked by more crooked motion and/or skipping over *svaras*. These particularly emotive and expressive phrases clearly depart from scalar structure and show Brinda's interpretive genius. For Activity 2.11 first copy the sequences of *svaras* given in the activity onto a blank piece of paper. Then as you listen to CD track 11, underline the *svaras* you hear being ornamented, indicating which of the three broad categories of ornament you would place them under. You will notice that the first time Viswanathan sings each phrase, he uses the *svara* names, while the second time he vocalizes with syllables such as *ta na na* or *na na na*; syllable sequences like this are typically used by singers in *ālāpana* improvisation.

ACTIVITY 2.11 *Phrases in Kīravāṇi Rāga (CD track 11)*

Characteristic Kīravāṇi phrases (0:00–0:42)

1. *ga ri ri , ri ,*
2. *ga pa ma ga ri, ri sa* $\underline{\textit{ni}}$ *,*
3. *sa* $\underline{\textit{ni}}$ *ri sa* $\underline{\textit{ni}}$ $\underline{\textit{dha}}$ *,*

Special Kīravāṇi phrases (0:44–1:27)

1. $\overline{\textit{ri}}$ *ni dha pa*
2. *ma \ * $\underline{\textit{ni}}$ *, sa ri ga ma*
3. *dha ni* $\overline{\textit{ri}}$ *ni dha pa ma*

Note: A comma indicates an extension of the previous svara or a pause approximately equal in duration to a voiced svara.

Phrases are extremely important in Kāpi rāga. Activity 2.12 (CD track 12) includes several examples of beautiful *vakra* motion and illustrates the use of notes "foreign" to the basic scale of the rāga, a practice more common in Hindustāni than Karṇāṭak music. In Kāpi rāga both the natural and flattened (major and minor) varieties of three *svaras* may occur: *ga, dha,* and *ni,* the third, sixth, and seventh degrees of the scale. Although the natural *ga* and flattened *dha* are not included in the basic scalar summary of the rāga given in Activity 2.9, they are used as occasional flavorings and are crucial to Kāpi's total *gestalt,* melodic identity. While two varieties each of *ga, dha,* and *ni* occur in performance, it cannot be stressed too strongly that each must be used in an appropriate context for the result to be perceived as Kāpi and not melodic chaos.

On CD track 12, Viswanathan sings selected phrases from the performance of the Kāpi rāga composition recorded by Bangalore Nagarathnammal and discussed in Chapter 4 (CD track 18), highlighting her juxtapositions of both varieties of *ga, dha,* and *ni.* As you listen, write on a piece of paper which *svaras* you hear rendered without ornamentation and which use each of the three types of ornament.

ACTIVITY 2.12 *Phrases in Kāpi Rāga (CD Track 12)*

Phrase 1: contains flat ga *and both varieties of* ni *(0:00–0:13)*
pa pa ma pa ni pa , ga , ri sa , ri ma ga ri sa ni sa
G G F G B♭ G , E♭ , D C , D F E♭ D C B C

Phrase 2: introduces natural ga *(0:14–0:25)*
pa ma ga, sa ga ma, ri ma pa dha ni ni dha dha pa ma ga, sa ga ma
G F E, C E F, D F G A B♭ B♭ A A G F E, C E F

Phrase 3: contains natural dha *and both varieties of* ni *(0:27–0:37)*
ri ma pa ni dha ni ma pa ni, s̄a, pa r̄i s̄a ni dha ni pa
D F G B♭ A B♭ F G B, C G D C B♭ A B♭ G

Phrase 4: introduces flat dha *(0:37–0:51)*
dha pa dha ma pa ga ri, sa ri pa ga ri, sa ni sa pa, ni, sa
A♭ G A♭ F G E♭ D, C D G E♭ D, C B♭ C G, B, C

Note: European note names are included, taking C as tonal center for purposes of convenience, to show varieties of svaras.

Natural and flattened varieties of both *ga* and *dha* are also clearly audible in the Kāpi rāga *bhajan* (CD track 1). In text line *B* of the *bhajan* (middle range of the melody) natural *ga* is followed by flattened *ga*, and text line *C* (upper range of the melody) contains natural *dha* followed by flattened *dha*.

*Functional Notes—*Svaras *Holding Particular Functions.* To invoke a comparison of the games of checkers and chess, while checkers are all the same shape and move in the same manner, chess pieces have different characters and functions—distinct types of potency and ways of moving. The *svaras* of a rāga are like chess pieces in that they can be quite distinct *types* of notes, serving different musical functions. The list of particular roles that can be fulfilled by a *svara* is long, and the meaning of many terms that appear in ancient treatises has changed or been lost over time, so assigning functional terms to particular *svaras* today is necessarily a somewhat subjective interpretive activity. The following are some of the terms used by Karṇāṭak musicians and theorists:

Jīva svara—life-giving or soul-giving *svara*

Graha svara—initial note, a *svara* used to begin melodic ideas

Nyāsa svara—ending note, a *svara* on which phrases come to rest

Dīrgha svara—a *svara* that is prolonged

Amśa svara—a *svara* that occurs frequently

Alpa svara—a *svara* voiced only sparingly or in passing

The functional term South Indian musicians use most often is *jīva svara*, the *svara* that gives life or soul to the rāga; as will become clear in Chapter 3, that function as well as several others are filled in Kīravāṇi rāga by *ri*.

INTEGRATED MELODIC-RHYTHMIC TRAINING

At this point we would like to show how the melodic and rhythmic principles discussed thus far are brought together in a student's training. The basic set of melodic-rhythmic exercises given to every beginning vocal student of Karṇāṭak music is called *saraḷi variśai*. Developed by the composer Purandara Dāsa in the sixteenth century, this graded series of exercises trains the student to be able to sing sequences of *svaras* in tune and in time (they are set to the eight-beat *ādi* tāḷa presented in

Activity 2.2). Because this set of exercises develops rhythmic and melodic skills *simultaneously*, we have found it an excellent resource for musicians, whatever their background or whatever styles they play. Many scales can be used as melodic material for the *saraḷi variśai*, the only requirement being that all seven *svaras* are used both in ascent and descent. Activity 2.13 presents scalar summaries of several well-known Karṇāṭak rāgas, which can then be used as the basis for the series of graded exercises in Activity 2.14.

The father of Karṇāṭak music. *Purandara Dāsa (1484–1564) is revered as the most important early figure in Karṇāṭak music. He composed hundreds of* gītams, *simple compositions that are a basic part of young students' training. One of these is* Śrī Gaṇanātha, *the song whose text is quoted at the beginning of this book. He developed systematic sets of melodic and rhythmic exercises and classified tāḷas into a coherent scheme. His compositions are sung in a range of contexts from Karṇāṭak concerts to regional folk performance (see discussion of* tatva *in Chapter 5), and his pedagogical exercises remain the basis of Karṇāṭak music training today.*

Practice singing the notes of the scales in Activity 2.13 in both ascending and descending directions, using the Karṇāṭak solfège names. As a background for your singing, try playing a steady melodic drone on your chosen tonal center (C is a common *sa* for male voices, F or G for women) using an electronic keyboard (you might tape down the appropriate keys to sustain the sound), a strummed open-tuned guitar, or other device of your own invention. Students traditionally begin study of saraḷi variśai with the first rāga on the list, Māyāmāḷavagauḷa.

ACTIVITY 2.13 *Scalar Summaries of Well-Known Karṇāṭak Rāgas and, Where Applicable, Their Equivalents in European Terminology*

	sa	ri	ga	ma	pa	dha	ni	ṡa
Māyāmāḷavagauḷa (basic first training scale; no equivalent European scale)	C	D♭	E	F	G	A♭	B	C′
Śaṅkarābharaṇam (Ionian mode/major scale)	C	D	E	F	G	A	B	C′
Kharaharapriya (Dorian mode)	C	D	E♭	F	G	A	B♭	C′
Tōḍī (Phrygian mode)	C	D♭	E♭	F	G	A♭	B♭	C′
Kalyāṇi (Lydian mode)	C	D	E	F♯	G	A	B	C′
Harikāmbhōji (Mixolydian mode)	C	D	E	F	G	A	B♭	C′
Naṭabhairavi (Aeolian mode)	C	D	E♭	F	G	A♭	B♭	C′
Kīravāṇi (harmonic minor)	C	D	E♭	F	G	A♭	B	C′
Hēmāvatī (no equivalent)	C	D	E♭	F♯	G	A	B♭	C′
Pantuvarāḷi (no equivalent)	C	D♭	E	F♯	G	A♭	B	C′

Note: All the rāgas presented here have the same seven svaras *in ascent and descent; to conserve space, only the ascending direction is given.*

Once you have familiarized yourself with singing some of the scales in Activity 2.13, go on to Activity 2.14. Here, the first seven exercises in the *saraḷi variśai* sequence are presented as taught by T. Viswanathan to his students. As an example, we have given the European pitch equivalents for Śaṅkarābharaṇam rāga underneath the line of *svaras*. Like the tāḷa exercises in Activities 2.3–2.5, these exercises are intended to be done in three speeds. For reasons of space, only the first speed (where one syllable equals one beat of the eight-beat *ādi* tāḷa) is shown. When you start singing in first speed, set the metronome to approximately 60 mm per beat of tāḷa (if you begin too quickly, you will not be able to do the exercise in second or third speed). To practice in second speed, double the rate at which you sing the *svaras*, while maintaining the tāḷa steadily; this will yield two *svaras* per beat of tāḷa. For third speed, again double the rate at which you sing the *svaras*, against your steady, unchanging counting of *ādi* tāḷa.

ACTIVITY 2.14 Saraḷi variśai *Exercises in Eight-Beat Ādi Tāla Illustrated in Śaṅkarābharaṇam Rāga (Its Scale Is Equivalent to the European Major Scale)*

Ādi *tāla:*
[beats]

```
1 2 3 4 5 6 7 8 - 1 2 3 4 5 6 7 8 - 1 2 3 4 5 6 7 8 - 1 2 3 4 5 6 7 8
```

[gestures]

```
C 2 3 4 C W C W - C 2 3 4 C W C W - C 2 3 4 C W C W - C 2 3 4 C W C W
```

Saraḷi variśai *exercises # 1–7 as taught by T. Viswanathan, in first speed:*

```
1. s r g m p d n s̄ - s̄ n d p m g r s - s r g m p d n s̄ - s̄ n d p m g r s
   C D E F G A B C - C B A G F E D C - C D E F G A B C - C B A G F E D C
2. s r s r s r g m   s r g m p d n s̄ - s̄ n s̄ n s̄ n d p   s̄ n d p m g r s
   C D C D C D E F   C D E F G A B C - C B C B C B A G   C B A D F E D C
3. s r g s r g s r   s r g m p d n s̄ - s̄ n d s̄ n d s̄ n   s̄ n d p m g r s
   C D E C D E C D   C D E F G A B C - C B A C B A C B   C B A G F E D C
4. s r g m s r g m   s r g m p d n s̄ - s̄ n d p s̄ n d p   s̄ n d p m g r s
   C D E F C D E F   C D E F G A B C - C B A G C B A G   C B A G F E D C
5. s r g m p , s r   s r g m p d n s̄ - s̄ n d p m , s̄ n   s̄ n d p m g r s
   C D E F G , C D   C D E F G A B C - C B A G F , C B   C B A G F E D C
6. s r g m p d s r   s r g m p d n s̄ - s̄ n d p m g s̄ n   s̄ n d p m g r s
   C D E F G A C D   C D E F G A B C - C B A G F E C B   C B A G F E D C
7. s r g m p s n ,   s r g m p d n s̄ - s̄ n d p m g r ,   s̄ n d p m g r s
   C D E F G A B ,   C D E F G A B C - C B A G F E D ,   C B A G F E D C
```

Note: Only the first letter of each svara *is used for space considerations; European note equivalents for Śaṅkarābharaṇam rāga are given below the* svaras, *taking C as tonal center for purposes of convenience.*

After practicing the exercises in Śaṅkarābharaṇam, try several other of the rāga scales. As a student progresses, the *guru* will begin to add appropriate ornamentation while singing the exercises; while it is an integral part of musical training, teaching *saraḷi variśai* with *gamaka* lays beyond the scope of our text.

SUMMARY

This chapter has introduced tāḷa and rāga, the crucial rhythmic and melodic parameters within which Karṇāṭak music operates. Activities have been structured to give the student a direct experience in becoming familiar with particular well-known rāgas and tāḷas found in musical compositions considered in the book and to illustrate how musicians think as they use these resources in composition and improvisation.

CHAPTER 3

The Karṇāṭak Concert Today

PRESENTATION AND DISCUSSION OF THE "MAIN PIECE" OF A CONCERT

This chapter demonstrates how a *kriti* can serve as the basis of an extended performance in a concert. What South Indians call the "main piece" of an evening's recital has been chosen for attention. A typical concert contains seven to ten *kritis*; in addition, concerts often begin with an etude-like piece called *tāna varṇam* and in the latter part contain one or two examples of the dance music genres *jāvaḷi* (CD track 18), *padam* (CD track 22), or *tillāna*. The main piece occurs usually a bit over halfway through a two-and-one-half- or three-hour concert, nested within a number of improvisational forms. This creates a performance of from twenty minutes to over an hour, comparable in length to most European symphonies.

The Setting. The performance in CD tracks 13–17 was recorded live at a house concert in the southern Chennai suburb of Besant Nagar on an autumn evening in 1977 (Figures 3.1–3.4). The audience was just a few feet from the performers, everyone sitting with legs crossed on a series of Persian rugs spread around the room. The featured performer was the eminent Karṇāṭak vocalist T. Brinda (also an accomplished performer on the lute *vīṇā*). For this concert, she was accompanied by her cousins T. Viswanathan on the *kuḻal* bamboo flute and his brother T. Ranganathan on the *mridaṅgam*, double-headed drum. The *tambūra* lute played by one of Brinda's students provided the background drone for the performance.

Many concerts are held today in large halls with microphones and amplification systems. A "mic-less" concert was chosen for this study partly because of its intimacy, which creates an environment conducive

FIGURE 3.1 *House in Besant Nagar neighborhood, Chennai, 1990.* *(Photograph by Matthew Allen)*

FIGURE 3.2 *Tree-lined street, Besant Nagar neighborhood, Chennai, 1990.* *(Photograph by Matthew Allen)*

FIGURE 3.3 *Fish vendors, Besant Nagar Second Main Road, Chennai, 1990.* *(Courtesy of Julie Searles)*

FIGURE 3.4 *Baskets for sale in front of* marundu kaḍai, *chemists' shops. Bazaar Road, Mylapore neighborhood, Chennai, 1990.* *(Courtesy of Julie Searles)*

to particularly good performances. On the CD audience members can be heard periodically humming along or keeping tāḷa with their hands. The intimate chamber recital (called *kaccēri,* "court," in Tamiḻ) dates back to the days of court and temple patronage in previous centuries in which, ideally, audience members were in their own way as educated as the performers. A well-informed sensitive listener is known as a *rasika,* someone who can taste the *rasa* (literally, "juice," aesthetic potential) inherent in the music.

Tuning Up. In Karṇāṭak music there is no concept of absolute pitch; the main artist chooses a tonic pitch (represented by the *svara sa,* analogous to the European *do*) well suited to his or her vocal range or instrument, and the *tambūra, mridaṅgam,* and violin accompanists base their tuning on the main artist's *sa.* While the choice is a personal one, many women sing at a *śruti* of between F and G (T. Brinda performed at F), and many men's *śruti* is around C. Working *mridaṅgam* players need to own many drums because the tuning of any one drum can only be altered by less than a minor second.

Karṇāṭak vocalists need to have a range of about two octaves. Much of the musical activity takes place within the *madhyama sthāyī,* central octave, but the range required to sing most compositions stretches into the adjacent octaves. Activity 3.1 involves finding a note that will serve as a good personal *sa,* tonal center, for your own vocal range. To do this, sit at a piano and find the lowest and highest notes that you can comfortably sing; the note approximately a perfect fourth above your lowest note, or the note a perfect fifth below your uppermost note, might be good candidates for your personal *sa.*

ACTIVITY 3.1 *Approximate Range Necessary for Performance of Karṇāṭak Music*

Lower octave	Central octave	Upper octave
$\underline{\text{pa}}$ $\underline{\text{dha}}$ $\underline{\text{ni}}$	sa ri ga ma pa dha ni	$\overline{\text{sa}}$ $\overline{\text{ri}}$ $\overline{\text{ga}}$ $\overline{\text{ma}}$ $\overline{\text{pa}}$

Beginning. The performance of "If It Was to Happen/Kaligiyuṇṭē" in CD tracks 13–17 is typical in that the ensemble did not rehearse beforehand, nor were the accompanists told what compositions would be on the recital before sitting down to play. Karṇāṭak musicians, like jazz performers, come to the stage with a knowledge of a repertoire of musical compositions, a set of processes by which these are interpreted in performance, and ears wide open. In both traditions, while musicians love to play with colleagues they know well, fine performances can also take place among musicians who have never even met, as long as they are familiar with the "standards" and the appropriate processes of interpretation and improvisation.

To join in when a *kriti* begins, Karṇāṭak accompanists need not know the particular composition but the *mridaṅgam* player must at least recognize the tāḷa, and the melodic accompanist must be familiar with the particular tāḷa and rāga. An accompanist may not be familiar with a soloist's particular *pāṭhāntara,* style of interpretation, of a piece, but she or he quickly adapts through close listening. When members of an ensemble know each other's repertoire and style intimately, as in the performance on CD tracks 13–17, the musical communication can become particularly profound and wonderful.

Kriti *as an Orally Transmitted Composed Core of a Performance.* To the student familiar with European art music, where composers commit their ideas to written form, the idea that composers exist in an oral tradition may not immediately make sense. The composed core of musical information given by a Karṇāṭak composer lives in the memory of musicians more than it does on paper, and compositions are always works in progress. In performance a mature performer interprets this fixed but flexible core, adding his or her own individual touches while staying faithful to the version learned from the *guru* and augmenting the composed core with various forms of improvisation.

BRIEF GUIDE TO THE PERFORMANCE (CD TRACKS 13–17)

A detailed discussion of the improvisational forms *ālāpana, niraval, svara kalpana,* and drum solo, and of the performance on CD tracks 13–17, including Activities and Listening Guides, is available at the URL http://www.wheatoncollege.edu/Faculty/MatthewAllen.html.

Composition and Improvisation: Fixity and Fluidity. A dialogue between what is fixed and what is created in the moment is at the heart of listeners' enjoyment of Karṇāṭak music. In this performance of *Kaligiyuṇṭē* four forms of *manōdharma,* improvisation (Viswanathan and Cormack 1998), envelop the central composed core, the *kriti.* While it is valid to draw a distinction between the *kriti* as composed and the other forms as improvised, it is important to remember that the *kriti* does contain flexibility in interpretation and that the improvised forms also contain much precomposed material, which serves as a basis for extemporization in performance. The performance of *Kaligiyuṇṭē* progresses through five stages.

1. *Ālāpana* (CD Track 13; 7:44): Unmetered melodic improvisation in the rāga
2. Kriti (CD Track 14; 6:28): Composed core of the performance
3. *Niraval* (CD Track 15; 5:25): Improvisation of melodic variations on a line from the *kriti*
4. *Svara kalpana* (CD Track 16; 5:13): Rhythmic/melodic improvisation using solfège syllables
5. *Tani āvarttanam* (CD Track 17; 3:55): Improvised drum solo played on the *mridaṅgam*

Kīravāṇi Rāga Ālāpana *(CD Track 13).* Brinda begins the performance with *ālāpana*, a melodic improvisation in free rhythm that introduces Kīravāṇi rāga to the audience and musicians alike. *Ālāpana* is performed at the beginning of about half of the *kritis* in a typical concert; it is at the discretion of the main artist to initiate *ālāpana*, or any other improvisational forms. Some *ālāpanas* are very brief, the main artist singing one or two characteristic phrases of the rāga, but for the main piece of a recital the *ālāpana* may easily last ten minutes or more. When a soloist performs *ālāpana* before a particular *kriti*, it is customary to give the melodic accompanist a turn to play an *ālāpana* as well. At the conclusion of *ālāpana*, the main performer leads the ensemble into a *kriti* set to the same rāga. One clue to recognizing *ālāpana* is that percussionists remain silent during this section (except for a few strokes on the drum between the vocal and flute *ālāpana* in CD track 13). Another clue is the lack of a texted line; singers use untexted vocables such as *ta da ri na* to voice the melody.

Aesthetics and Dynamics of Accompaniment. As Brinda sings *ālāpana*, Viswanathan begins to accompany her on the *kuḻal* bamboo flute. As the melodic accompanist in this concert, his job in the *ālāpana* and throughout the performance is to support—not upstage or overshadow—the main artist. Brinda initiates the melodic ideas and Viswanathan responds, echoing the ends of her phrases or sometimes playing sustained tones in the background. As he plays, Viswanathan does not directly imitate Brinda's singing; rather, in heterophonic fashion he fills out the

FIGURE 3.5 *Photograph of T. Brinda, Chennai, 1990.* *(Courtesy of Julie Searles)*

total sound, adding his own perspective on her vocal line in a subtle and restrained manner.

At the conclusion of her *ālāpana* Brinda motions to Viswanathan that she would like him to play *ālāpana* before she begins singing the *kriti* (at this point the drummer T. Ranganathan plays a few strokes on his *mridaṅgam* to check that it is properly tuned). Viswanathan then performs a brief (1:30) *ālāpana*. For this performance he did not have a flute in Brinda's tonic pitch F, so he played a C flute in transposition. Having to instantly transpose everything by a perfect fifth was one factor that led him to keep his *ālāpana* relatively brief; he also felt that Brinda had already given a thorough introduction to the rāga. A detailed description of CD track 13, including activities for students, is available at http://www.wheatoncollege.edu/Faculty/MatthewAllen.html.

∞

> A note with several important functions. *It quickly becomes clear that the* svara ri *is extremely important in Kīravāṇi rāga. Brinda's first* ālāpana *phrase is* ga ri ri , ri , *(phrase 1 in Activity 2:11), illustrating how* ri *is both a* nyāsa *(ending) and a* dīrgha *(prolonged)* svara *for Kīravāṇi. Taking Brinda's* ālāpana *improvisation as a whole,*

it becomes clear why musicians also identify ri *as the* jīva svara *of Kīravāṇi, the* svara *that most gives it life and soul.*

Kriti: ***The Core Component (CD Track 14).*** When Viswanathan finishes his *ālāpana* and Brinda begins the *kriti*, an unmistakable acoustic event occurs—the *mridaṅgam* begins accompanying. The beginning of the *kriti* also marks the entry of the tāḷa. Drummer T. Ranganathan waits for Brinda to begin the first line of the *pallavi* section of the *kriti*. He listens carefully to get a "fix" on the tempo she has chosen and then begins to play. From here to the end of the performance, the cycles of eight-beat *ādi* tāḷa go round and round.

While Muttuttandavar (CD track 3) expressed his devotion to Naṭarāja, Tyagaraja's chosen personal deity was Rāma. Hindu composers and poets express their *bhakti*, devotion, in many ways. Tyagaraja usually addresses Rāma directly, personally, and emotionally, pleading with, sometimes even cajoling, Rāma to protect and save him. This is quite unlike the more formal approach to *bhakti* taken by composers such as Tyagaraja's contemporary Muttusvami Dikshitar, whose *kriti* texts often focused on detailed description of the physical appearance of deities and the rituals performed for them at particular temples.

On the process of translation. *Telugu scholar Phillip Wagoner translated three Telugu compositions for this book. Asked for his comments on how the Telugu language works in this particular text, he sent this response: "Apart from the usual richness of meaning generated by the repetition of the* pallavi *and its slight shifts as it construes with the* anupallavi *or* caraṇam, *there also seems to be a deeper tug going on between the idea of the inevitability of fate and God's ability to override fate. Thus, in the* pallavi, *the first line is wholly fatalistic (although a little window of doubt is cast by* gadā, *'isn't it?'), while the second line declares that God has the power to grant what is desired. This makes for an intriguing tension throughout the rest of the song: Tyagaraja is absolved from guilt for criticizing God because it was fated to happen; but then in the* caraṇam, *he wistfully wants to have his fate changed so he can be like the devotees of yore" (personal communication 2001).*

ACTIVITY 3.2 *Text and Translation of* Kriti *"If It Was to Happen/*Kaligiyuṇṭē*" (CD Track 14)*

Rāga: Kiravāṇi; Tāḷa: ādi *(eight-beat cycle); T. Brinda, vocalist; T. Viswanathan, flute; T. Ranganathan,* mridaṅgam

Pallavi (close translation):	(Freer translation):
Kaligiyuṇṭē gadā galgunu	
If it was to happen—no?—it happens	What is to happen will happen—
Kāmita phala dāyaka	
O giver of desired fruit	Isn't that right, O you who grant our desires?
Anupallavi:	
Kalini ingitam erugaka ninnu āḍukonṭi	
In this Kali age, not knowing good sense, I blamed you	In this age of ignorance I lost my sense, and I blamed you
Calamu sēyaka nā talanu cakkani vrāta	
But not out of malice; that fate [was] written right on my forehead	Don't be angry with me—That fate was written right on my brow
Caraṇam:	
Bhāgavata agrēsarulu agu nārada	
The way in which the great devotees Nārada,	Those bygone devotees Nārada,
Prahlāda parāśara rāmadāsulu	
Prahlāda, Parāsara, and Rāmadas	Prahlāda, Parāsara, and Rāmadas
Bāguga śrī raghu rāmuni pādamulan	
Worshiped Raghu Rāma's feet so well	Knew how to worship you well
Bhakti jēsina rīti tyāgarājuniku ippuḍu	
[Make that be] for Tyagaraja now	If only their way could be Tyagaraja's now

[Translated from the Telugu by Phillip B. Wagoner]

The Pallavi *(CD Track 14, 0:00–2:11).* The text of a *pallavi* section provides the central seed thought of a *kriti*—remember its meaning, "sprouting"—the thought that the listener first encounters and that then returns after both the *anupallavi* and *caraṇam* sections. Brinda sings the first line of the *pallavi* six times before going to the second line. By the sixth time, she has made the line ornamentally more complex, but in such a subtle way that it takes close attention to notice. The multiple hearings of this line give the opportunity to become familiar with it and aid in recognizing the *pallavi's* reappearance later in the *kriti.*

The Anupallavi *and* Pallavi *reprise (CD Track 14, 2:12–4:09).* The *anupallavi* forms the melodic climax of most *kritis,* as here the melody moves into the upper octave. In *anupallavi* the text often reaches a high point of intensity as well. In *Kaligiyuṇṭē,* Tyagaraja pleads with Rāma to forgive him for his failings, then folds his thought back into the text of the *pallavi* by saying, "Unless fate has written it on my head . . . will I receive your blessing?" Brinda moves through the *anupallavi* in much the same way she sings the *pallavi*: She sings the first line four times, with a melodic variation on the word *ingitam* the last two times. Brinda sings the second line three times, adding a subtle variation on *nā* the second and third time, before returning to the *pallavi* reprise. In the brief reprise, the *pallavi* text takes on new meaning because the *anupallavi* has revealed more about Tyagaraja's emotional state.

The Caraṇam *and* Pallavi *Reprise (CD Track 14, 4:10–6:28).* The *caraṇam* has four text lines, twice as many as either *pallavi* or *anupallavi.* This is a very common proportion for *kriti* texts. As in many *caraṇams,* the melody of the first two lines settles into the middle part of the central octave. In the last two lines of the *caraṇam* of *Kaligiyuṇṭē* two things happen that occur in almost all of Tyagaraja's *kritis.* First, the upper register melody from the *anupallavi* is used to set the third and fourth lines of the *caraṇam.* Then at the end of the last line, the composer has inserted his name into the text; this is his *mudrā,* signature. At the end of the *caraṇam,* as at the end of the *anupallavi,* Brinda leads the ensemble back through the reprise of the *pallavi.* A detailed description of CD track 14 including listening guide and activities for students is available at http://www.wheatoncollege.edu/Faculty/MatthewAllen.html.

Niraval *(CD Track 15).* *Niraval* is an improvisation in which the main artist spontaneously improvises a new melodic setting for a particular line of a *kriti* several times in succession, while keeping the rhythmic structure of the chosen line of text intact (or almost intact—some flexibility is allowed). The line is usually taken from the *caraṇam,* but it may also be from the *anupallavi*. In this performance, Brinda chooses the first line of the *caraṇam* text to render *niraval*. When she shifts to the next form of improvisation, *svara kalpana*, she will use the first phrase of the same text line as her theme of return. She begins *niraval* by singing the first words of the line; then, with responses from the flutist Viswanathan at each stage of the way, improvises a total of eight successive turns or "rounds." A detailed description of CD track 15 is available at http://www.wheatoncollege.edu/Faculty/MatthewAllen.html.

Svara Kalpana ***(CD Track 16)*** After Viswanathan's flute response to Brinda's final round of *niraval*, she immediately begins the next improvisational form, *svara kalpana* ("invented" or "created" *svaras*), initiating a series of interchanges based on the Karṇāṭak solfège syllables. When the soloist is a vocalist, as on this recording, it is easy to recognize the beginning of *svara kalpana* because the short staccato syllables sound distinctly different from the melismatic Telugu setting of the *kriti* text, even to one unfamiliar with the language. The soloist begins *svara kalpana* by improvising a melodic passage in solfège syllables, calculating it to end at the right moment and correct pitch to return seamlessly to the beginning of a composed line of the *kriti* chosen as a momentary theme of return. In this performance Ms. Brinda uses the first two words of the first line of the *caraṇam* as the theme of return, the same line she has just used for *niraval* improvisation. A detailed description of CD track 16 is available at http://www.wheatoncollege.edu/Faculty/MatthewAllen.html.

Different Ways to Improvise: A Comparison of Niraval *and* Svara Kalpana. *Svara kalpana* and *niraval* both involve a call-and-response dialogue between the main artist and melodic accompanist, but the form of the call-and-response differs between the two. In *niraval*, the soloist and accompanist take at least one or two cycles of tāḷa at a time for their improvisations; in *svara kalpana*, from one round to the next the *svara* phrases grow progressively longer in small increments—in general increasing by numbers of beats, not by whole cycles of tāḷa.

The feeling of a playful contest that the listener may begin to sense in *niraval* emerges as a clear focus of *svara kalpana*. The challenge for the melodic accompanist is to respond to the main artist's solfege improvisation immediately with a complementary musical line, having only heard the soloist's improvisation once and in a very fleeting manner. The accompanist's response should show that she or he has intuitively grasped the structure of the main artist's improvisation, but it should not attempt to overshadow the main artist by issuing challenges in return. An accompanist who "shows up" a main artist is not offered the opportunity to accompany that artist again. When the accompanist's response is finished, the soloist initiates another round, the process continuing until the soloist decides to move to the next section of the piece.

Calculating, floating, and adjusting. *While* kaṇakku, *calculation, is an important component of svara kalpana, it is only part of the picture. Ethnomusicologist and violinist Amanda Weidman writes: "Most of what goes on in* svara kalpana *is not strictly calculated or premeditated. Musicians develop their own habits for passing musical time, quasi-formulaic ways of floating that are known to take a certain amount of time, habits that are as much bodily as mental. Unlike Western ideas of improvisation as the expression of musical ideas, the Karṇāṭak sense of "improvisation" in* svara kalpana *is of filling tāḷa cycles. But there will also be parts where a musician completely loses track of the tāḷa, playing or singing lyrically, and then gradually coming back into calculation, "adjusting" (the English term is used) until he can find or intuit the correct place to start the ending literally calculated to thrill the audience. One becomes able to do* svara kalpana *not because one can calculate, but because one can adjust" (Weidman 2001:32).*

There are strong structural similarities between Brinda's *niraval* and *svara kalpana* improvisations in CD tracks 15 and 16. She does eight rounds of improvisation in each. The first five rounds of both are in slow tempo, the fifth round being particularly expansive, with many beautiful rāga phrases worked into both vocal and flute improvisations. The final three rounds of both her *niraval* and her *svara kalpana* are in *madhyama kāla,* where the rhythmic density of *svaras* is doubled. During the final three rounds of *svara kalpana* the energy and intensity build as the *svaras* come twice as fast and T. Ranganathan correspondingly increases the density of his *mridaṅgam* accompaniment. At the conclusion of Viswanathan's eighth round, Ranganathan finishes off the section with a rhythmic cadence, leading to enthusiastic applause from the audience members. The stage is now set for the final portion of the performance, the drum solo.

Tani Āvarttanam—*Drum Solo (CD Track 17).* In every Karṇāṭak concert the percussionist has one opportunity to take an extended solo, which may be from two to over twenty minutes in length. A few observations may help the listener keep tāḷa and follow its progress. At the beginning of Ranganathan's solo in CD track 17, his third stroke on the *mridaṅgam* coincides with the *samam*, the first beat of the tāḷa. From this point on, audience members can be heard clapping along on the first, fifth, and seventh beats of the tāḷa cycle. A *mridaṅgam* solo balances two basic modes of rhythmic thinking: *sarva laghu*, time flow, and *kaṇakku*, calculation. The student of *mridaṅgam* must learn both to be able to flow with the music in a sensitive manner and to calculate and manipulate complex rhythmic patterns. *Sarva laghu* includes patterns and quasi-melodic figures that reinforce the flow of the tāḷa. "Karṇāṭak drummers devise their time-flow figures as much for their pleasing sound as for their rhythmic effect. A listener will find it relatively easy to keep the tāḷa during sections that emphasize this type of playing. These patterns may be compared with others found in drumming throughout the world: the ride cymbal patterns used by jazz drummers, the complex yet flowing patterns of African-Latin drummers, and the patterns employed by players of the Irish frame drum (*bodhran*) are all analogous to the time flow of Karṇāṭak drummers" (Nelson, in Arnold 2000:153).

In the second mode, *kaṇakku*, calculation, a drummer designs patterns that disrupt the smooth steady progress through the tāḷa in such a way that the novice listener can easily become lost. "A listener may know that one of these designs is unfolding by noticing that the tāḷa has suddenly become hard to follow. Some sort of rhythmic shape emerges, but its relationship with the beat seems tense. When it resolves, informed listeners, including the other performers, may nod their approval or briefly applaud" (Nelson, in Arnold 2000:154).

A full-length *mridaṅgam* solo usually moves through three sections (Activity 3.3). When, as on CD Track 17, a solo is brief, the drummer will often skip the first section, beginning with medium tempo time flow figures characteristic of the second section of a solo. A detailed description of CD track 17 is available at http://www.wheatoncollege.edu/Faculty/MatthewAllen.html.

ACTIVITY 3.3 *Structure of a Typical* Mridangam *Solo*

First section	Second section (0:00–2:18 on CD Track 17)	Third section (2:18–3:50 on Track 17)
Sparsely articulated slow tempo time flow figures lead to cadential pattern	Medium tempo time flow figures lead to pattern; usually the longest section	Dense high-speed patterns lead to final cadential pattern

SUMMARY

This chapter has illustrated how a *kriti*, augmented with several forms of improvisation, becomes a multi-chambered musical form and the centerpiece of a Karṇāṭak concert. Composed and improvised forms have been clearly distinguished; at the same time, the flexibility of interpretation possible in composed music and the formal structures on which improvised forms are based have also been stressed. Additional listening guides and activities, available at coauthor Allen's website, have been designed to give the student a basic understanding of the inner workings of improvisatory forms in Karṇāṭak music and to enable the listener to appreciate the recorded performance on CD Tracks 13–17.

CHAPTER 4

Contextualizing South Indian Performance, Socially and Historically

WOMEN AND MUSIC: THE *DĒVADĀSI* AND HER COMMUNITY

To begin, a question. When listening to the main piece *Kaligiyuṇṭē* (CD tracks 13–17) did it strike you as significant that the main artist—choosing the repertoire, initiating all the improvisational forms, making key decisions at every stage about the progress of the concert—is a woman? As recently as seventy years ago, this scenario simply could not have taken place because women's and men's performance traditions were quite distinct at the beginning of the twentieth century.

There were many women musicians in South India around 1900—mostly vocalists, some performers of the chordophone *vīṇā*, and a few violinists and percussionists. But women who performed Karṇāṭak music in public were not from all classes of society; they belonged almost completely to one particular social community. As early as the Cōḻa dynasty in South India (ca. ninth through eleventh centuries A.D.), and perhaps much earlier (Figure 4.1), a class of women famous for their music and dance skills was attached in hereditary service to both Hindu temples and the royal courts. Called *dēvadāsi* (literally, servants, *dāsi*, of god, *dēva*), young women of this community were ritually married to the god of a particular Hindu temple. For the more artistically promising girls, this marriage and their artistic *araṅgēṟṟam*, debut, came at the conclusion of a period of training in music and dance. In temple service they performed both artistic and specifically ritual functions, and particularly accomplished *dēvadāsis* often performed in the court setting

FIGURE 4.1 *Replica of bronze statuette (10.8 cm in height), Mohenjo Daro civilization, circa 2500* B.C. *Original in National Museum, Delhi.* *(Photograph by Matthew Allen)*

for the king and royal family as well. Because of their marriage to god, they were considered *nityāsumaṅgaḷī*, "ever-auspicious" women, because unlike human husbands, gods do not die, so *dēvadāsis* avoided the traditionally inauspicious state of widowhood (Kersenboom 1987). In temple service *dēvadāsis* had a set of ritual responsibilities only they were qualified to perform. Many *dēvadāsis* were literate, having a level of education that women of higher social status were denied. *Dēvadāsis* lived outside of the institution of human marriage and bore children by patrons who in many cases were lifelong companions. Many owned considerable property and are mentioned in historical sources not only as great dancers and musicians but as authors and philanthropists as well.

During the nineteenth century, when the British consolidated their control over India, *dēvadāsis* were still attached to temples and remaining courts throughout the South. They were particularly renowned for their performance of dance in a style called at that time *sadir* or *nautch* (an Anglicization of the Sanskrit *nāṭya*, "drama-dance-music"). In 1799 the British took control of most revenues from the kingdom of Tañjāvūr and in 1855, upon the death of Rāja Sivaji II without male issue, assumed direct rule. This accelerated the decline of the system of patronage that had supported *dēvadāsis* and other temple service castes since the Cōḻa period. By the beginning of the twentieth century, no indigenous royal house remained to support the temples, which had provided *dēvadāsis* with housing and food. Many *dēvadāsis* lost their livelihood and homes, some turning to prostitution. Because of this, *dēvadāsis* were viewed in general as prostitutes by the Victorian-educated Indian middle and upper classes, and their dance was seen as degraded, not fit for respectable company.

> The death of the dēvadāsi and the "revival" of her dance in a new social milieu. *In a profound early twentieth-century social transformation, women of the hereditary community almost completely gave up dance in favor of professions not tainted by social stigma (performance of vocal music offered one such outlet). The temple dedication of young women as* dēvadāsis *was prohibited by law in Tamiḻ Nāḍu in 1947, ending a social and cultural tradition over a millennium old. The* dēvadāsis' *dance was renamed* bharata nāṭyam *(loosely translatable as the "complete theatrical art of India") and repopulated, primarily by women from the Brahmin community (Allen 1997, Meduri 2001).*

Women's Public Performance Circa 1900. In the first two decades of the twentieth century, women of *dēvadāsi* community background were the only women performing Karṇāṭak music in public. Their performances were distinctly different in form and content from those of men. Women's performances featured the presentation of many com-

FIGURE 4.2 *Sisters T. Brinda (holding* tambūra *across her lap), T. Muktha, and T. Abhiramasundari (with violin), 1942. (Courtesy of T. Muktha)*

positions and relatively little improvisation except for *ālāpana*. Women were known as repositories of *kritis* and also genres from the dance repertoire such as *jāvaḷis* and *padams* (examples on CD tracks 18 and 22). Concerts by women singers stressed harmonious ensemble performance rather than the jousting improvisational back-and-forth affiliated with improvisation and gendered as male musical behavior. Embodying the idea of a close-knit ensemble, sister duets or trios were common. T. Brinda's aunts Rajalakshmi and Lakshmiratnam performed in their youth as "Dhanam's Daughters," and Brinda herself performed for many years with her younger sisters, vocalist T. Muktha and violinist T. Abhiramasundari (Figure 4.2).

Social attitudes of the time discouraged women from performance of improvised music and from mannerisms considered male, such as the keeping of *tāḷa* on the thighs: In the words of Brinda's grandmother Vina Dhanammal, "Women should not be slapping their thighs like men!" It was also a common perception that women's voices retained their naturally sweet character into maturity, while men's became "hardened" by strenuous *svara* singing.

Loss and Recovery of a Woman's Work. Despite women's participation in artistic life from time immemorial, written accounts of South Indian music and literary history have tended to concentrate on the contributions of men. When work by or about women musicians, authors, or composers has been published, in some cases it has been deliberately altered, in effect erased and suppressed. The life of Muddupalani, a *dēvadāsi* poet at the Tañjāvūr Court during the reign of Rāja Pratap Singh (1739–1763), is a striking case in point. Among her Telugu works is an epic poem, *Radhika Santwanam,* "Appeasing Rādhā," her own telling of a story known to all Indians, the romance of Rādhā and Kṛṣṇa. While scholars agree that her work is a sophisticated and polished piece of poetry, something else makes it especially remarkable to literary historians Susie Tharu and K. Lalita:

> What strikes us today is Muddupalani's remarkable subversions of the received form. Traditionally in such literature, the man is the lover, the woman the loved one; Krishna woos and makes love to Radha. Though Radha is invariably portrayed as longing for him, the narrative has as its focus his pleasure. Not so in *Radhika Santwanam,* where the woman's sensuality is central. She takes the initiative, and it is her satisfaction or pleasure that provides the poetic resolution. With a warmth unmatched in later poetry, Muddupalani celebrates a young girl's coming of age and describes her first experience of sex. . . . What makes the work so radical today, if not in its own time, is the easy confidence with which it contests the asymmetries of sexual satisfaction commonly accepted even today, and asserts women's claim to pleasure. (Tharu and Lalita 1991:7)

Muddupalani's poem was published in 1887 by Venkatanarasu, an associate of the Orientalist lexicographer C. P. Brown. He excised not only verses he found objectionably erotic but also Muddupalani's prologue in which she introduced herself and discussed her literary lineage through her grandmother and aunt, themselves poets. The author's gender as well as her lineage were thus concealed.

Bangalore Nagarathnammal (1878–1952), the most popular woman vocalist of the early twentieth century, an accomplished Sanskrit scholar and proudly self-proclaimed *dēvadāsi*, first heard of Muddupalani while reading a commentary on the Tañjāvūr period of Telugu literature. Her interest was piqued by some extracts from the poems, and she began a search for *Radhika Santwanam* that eventually led her to a copy of the original manuscript. After comparing it with the 1887 edition, she decided to publish a new edition, restoring all the verses that had been left out. In her introduction to that edition she wrote: "However often I read this book, I feel like reading it all over again. . . . Since this poem, brimming with *rasa* [flavor, emotion] was not only written by a woman, but by one who was born into our community, I felt it necessary to publish it in its proper form" (in Tharu and Lalita 1991:2–3).

Nagarathnammal brought out her new edition of Muddupalani's poem in 1910 through Vavilla Ramaswami Sastrulu and Sons, one of the oldest and most reputable publishers in Chennai. To the amazement and consternation of Nagarathnammal and the publishers, several prominent social reformers denounced Muddupalani as an adulteress and her work as scandalous, leading the British government to seize all copies of the book and ban its publication. All petitions by Nagarathnammal and the publishers, including one to have a Telugu-speaking judge review the case, were dismissed. Clandestine copies circulated until the ban was lifted in 1947, the year of India's independence, and a new edition was published in 1952.

"Now We Women Have a Platform to Commence Singing"—Bangalore Nagarathnammal and the Tyagaraja Festival. The recovery of Muddupalani's work was only one of many philanthropic activities of Nagarathnammal. In 1921, her *guru* Bidaram Krishnappa sent her a letter saying how distraught he had been to see the dilapidated condition of Tyagaraja's shrine on a recent visit to Tiruvaiyāṟu, and asking her to dedicate herself to its renovation. She immediately took the train to Tiruvaiyāṟu and brought her considerable financial resources to bear on the situation. She found a sculptor to make stone images of Tyagaraja and the deity Hanumān for the shrine. Descendants of the last Rāja of Tañjāvūr exchanged their lands at the site with nearby properties purchased by Nagarathnammal, enabling her to construct a new auditorium with a large seating capacity; it is used to this day during the Tyagaraja *ārādhana* celebration. Consecration of the newly renovated shrine took place in 1925. As owner of the land, Nagarathnammal was in a position to insist that women, not previously allowed to make a musical offering during the Tyagaraja festival, participate alongside men. She declared: "Now we women have a platform to commence singing."

Nagarathnammal continued her intimate involvement with the Tyagaraja celebration until her death in 1952, establishing a trust to ensure that after her death the property would be maintained properly and that observances would be open to people of all social classes. In her will she insisted that her own mausoleum be positioned close to Tyagaraja's shrine to enable her always to have *darśan*, sight, of the composer she revered (on the importance of *darśan*, see Eck 1998). The carpenters who build the temporary performance platform for the festival every year obey her wish by placing it so that Tyagaraja and his great female devotee can have direct visual contact in perpetuity (for a summary of Nagarathnammal's life, see Jackson 1994:145–163).

Bangalore Nagarathnammal as a Performer. It was Bangalore Nagarathnammal's successful career as a singer and recording artist that made possible her philanthropic work. A catalogue of her performances between 1905 and 1934 lists 1,235 concerts in 116 different cities (Sankaran and Allen, in Arnold 2000:392). When George Walter Dillnutt of The Gramophone Company of India, Ltd, recorded her singing the *jāvaḷi* dance composition *"Didn't I Tell You Not To, Girl/Vaddani?"* (CD track 18) in Bangalore in late 1921, she was at the height of her popularity (the recording was released in March 1923; Michael Kinnear, personal communication December 9, 2002). Like most women of *dēvadāsi* background in the early twentieth century, the women in her family had stopped dancing; performing as a singer remained a route open to these women to gain a living with less social censure. And as with many other women singers of *dēvadāsi* background in the 1920s and 1930s who made 78 RPM recordings, many of Nagarathnammal's recordings are of dance music compositions.

Śringāra Bhakti: *Being in Love with God.* The dance music genres *jāvaḷi* and *padam,* dealing as they do with the myriad varieties of love in separation, are excellent vehicles for the portrayal of the *śringāra rasa,* erotic sentiment, in dance. These genres were at the heart of the performance repertoire of women from the *dēvadāsi* community. Most of the texts are constructed around a triad of characters: the hero (usually truant or otherwise absent), the heroine (usually pining, often with a barely concealed subcurrent of righteous anger), and the *sakhī*, the heroine's female friend and confidante (who sometimes ends up in the arms of the hero to whom she has gone on the behalf of the heroine) or female relative. A study of thirty Tamiḻ language *padams* by co-author Allen found that in almost half, the heroine addresses her confidante about her separation from the hero. Translations of the *pallavi* sections of six such *padams* are given here.

Spoken by the heroine to her friend:
Who will carry my message to him? Can I find a trustworthy confidante?
Wherever he has gone, my friend, he must still be thinking of me.
Oh friend, which woman could have poisoned his mind against me?
From now on, between him and me there can be no reconciliation—go, friend!
Without understanding, I fell in love with him—but what result did I see?
Oh my friend, can I ever forget his deceit? But at the same time, how can I not think of our sweet embraces? (Allen 1992:298)

In a smaller number of songs, the rhetoric of address is different: The confidante speaks, either to the heroine (as in the *jāvaḷi*, CD track 18) or to the hero on behalf of the heroine; and very occasionally, the heroine addresses the hero directly. For a dancer, who in the course of a performance uses her *abhināya*, mimetic gesture language, to bring to life all three characters—heroine, confidante, and hero—these songs are extremely rich in interpretive possibilities (Figure 4.3). In performance a dancer often improvises multiple interpretations of individual text lines

FIGURE 4.3 *Photograph of* bharata nāṭyam *dancer Lakshmi Shanmukham Knight with T. Viswanathan, flute; John Suter,* tambūra; *Jody Cormack Viswanathan, voice; Douglas Knight,* mridaṅgam. *(Courtesy of Jody Cormack Viswanathan)*

so that in concert a *padam* or *jāvaḷi* may last easily fifteen minutes, much longer than the recording on CD track 18.

One of the major ways that Hindu *bhakti* has been expressed throughout the centuries is through the dynamic of lover-beloved, the human devotee falling hopelessly in love with the deity (Cutler 1987:1). While the hero of most *padams* is identified as a deity—Kṛṣṇa and Murugan (one of Śiva's sons) are most often invoked—and thus these love songs are considered allegories for religious devotion, many *jāvaḷis* are addressed to human patrons. In *padams*, the tone of the love relationship is therefore generally considered more decorous than in *jāvaḷis*, which are often extremely direct in the portrayal of the relationship between lover and beloved (Ramanujan et al. 1994). Historically, *dēvadāsi* dancers performed these songs both for the deities in the temples where they served and in salons or courts in front of human patrons. Their always passionate, sometimes quite earthy and direct, texts served both to make these songs extremely popular and, by the late nineteenth century, to draw down upon them and their human practitioners the venom of social reformers.

In Activity 4.1, first study the text, in which the confidante (her friend, or perhaps her mother?) counsels the heroine, and then rewrite it from the point of view of one of the two other protagonists—the wronged heroine or the allegedly duplicitous hero. As you compose your lyric, keep in mind that a text that is too literal and detailed leaves little room for creative interpretation by a dancer; make your text sparse and suggestive rather than lengthy and descriptive. The structure of both *padam* and *jāvaḷi* is identical to *kriti*, each having the same three sections: *pallavi, anupallavi, caraṇam.*

ACTIVITY 4.1 *Text and Translation of* "Didn't I Tell You Not To, Girl/Vaddani?" *(CD Track 18)*
Composed by Mysore Venkatarama Sastri (nineteenth century)
Rāga: Kāpi; Tāḷa: rūpaka (three-beat cycle); Bangalore Nagarathnammal, vocalist; violin and mridaṅgam, *unknown*

Pallavi (begins at 0:00)

Vaddani nēnaṇṭini gā vāni	Didn't I tell you not to, girl?
(Vāni) jōli nīku celi	Not to have anything to do with him?

Anupallavi (begins at 0:43)

Sadayu mōsakāḍanē	He pretends to be nice, but look
Vāḍevvatanō jērināḍē	He's already involved with someone else

Caraṇam (begins at 1:36)

Cukkapu doravalenu cāla vakkaṇagā māṭalāḍucu	Like some slick lord, he talks politely
Nakkavinayamunu jēsē ṭakkaritō sahavāsamu	But he goes and acts just like a fox; don't get involved with a rogue like him.

[Translated from the Telugu by Phillip B. Wagoner]

Like the *bhajan* (CD track 1), "Didn't I Tell You Not To, Girl?" (CD track 18) is set to Kāpi rāga. Refresh your memory on the structure and important phrases of this rāga by referring back to CD track 9 and Activity 2.9. This composition is set to a very brisk three-beat *rūpaka* tāḷa. Before listening to CD track 18, recite the first line of the *pallavi* (Activity 4.2) while keeping the clap-clap-wave pattern of *rūpaka* tāḷa. Notice that this line is three cycles of tāḷa in length; as you listen to the complete recording, notice the different number of cycles of tāḷa taken by different lines in the *anupallavi* and *caraṇam* sections. A detailed listening guide to CD track 18 is available at http://www.wheatoncollege.edu/Faculty/MatthewAllen.html.

ACTIVITY 4.2 *Recitation of first line of* Pallavi *of* "Didn't I Tell You Not To, Girl/Vaddani?" *in* Rūpaka *Tāḷa (CD Track 18)*

1	2	3	1	2	3	1	2	3
clap	clap	wave	clap	clap	wave	clap	clap	wave
vad	dani	nē	naṇ	ṭini	gā -	- vā	ni	,

Listening through the Static: The Rise of Audio Recording. How can one enjoy music that sounds so scratchy, indistinct, and faraway? The first commercial gramophone recordings, manufactured on ten-inch plates, were being sold in India by 1910. In the 1920s 78 RPM records became the norm, and in the early 1930s the new electrical system of recording came to India from the United Kingdom. Recorded in 1921, CD track 18 certainly sounds far from high-fidelity to our twenty-first century ears. Once you have practiced reciting the *pallavi* line together with the tāḷa in Activity 4.2, our next suggestion is to get involved in the performance by clapping the cycles of *rūpaka* tāḷa with hand gestures as you listen—the cycle begins right at the singer's first syllable *vad*. The (unidentified) drummer's accompaniment is bursting with energy and is extremely creative; listen, for example, to how his crisp cadences resolve at the beginning of particular tāḷa cycles. As you clap, close your eyes and try to visualize the musicians playing. See if this begins to pull you through the haze of time into their presence, seated in front of a microphone one day over three quarters of a century ago.

The singer, Nagarathnammal, also adds many individual touches to this particular performance that can draw the listener in. You may have noticed how she introduces the first line of the *pallavi* into the *anupallavi* and *caraṇam* sections—anticipating the return of the *pallavi* section and in effect blurring the distinctions between the three parts of the song. Her fast *brikka* passages up and down the scale of the rāga (from 1:53 to 2:06) are a clear demonstration of the skills that made her such a popular singer. And it is quite remarkable to hear Nagarathnammal perform *ālāpana* for the *last* twenty seconds or so of the recording! This inversion of the normal sequence—where *ālāpana* precedes the composition—was necessitated by the recording format. After drastically curtailing their performance to fit the limitations of the technology, just over three minutes per side, musicians sometimes finished a composition with a few seconds to spare and opted to fill the remaining time with a brief spontaneous *ālāpana*.

MEN AND MUSIC: FROM TEMPLE AND COURT TO PUBLIC AND STATE PATRONAGE

At the beginning of the twentieth century the world of courtly patronage was nearly gone. Some Rājas—in South India, at Pudukkottai, Travancore, and Mysore—retained titles, palaces, and a retinue, although not political power. Some wealthy *zamindārs*, landowners, tried to emulate a courtly style of patronage in their private salons. But crucially, new performance contexts and patrons were emerging—especially the public concert, open to the public by paid admission, and the state, primarily through the new medium of the radio.

Men's Performance in Precolonial South India. Quintessential male performance in the old courtly context was *manōdharma saṅgīta*, improvised music. Male musicians from both Brahmin and non-Brahmin social classes gained formidable reputations for their improvisational skills. The musical genre par excellence was not the heavily texted devotional *kriti* but rather the *rāgam-tānam-pallavi* (often called simply *pallavi*), consisting of several improvisational genres spun in sequence around a brief composed core theme—usually just one line of text. The first part of the *rāgam-tānam-pallavi* consisted of extensive *rāga ālāpana*. Musicians' reputations were built on the rendition of particular rāgas: A musician associated with a particular rāga might acquire it as a nickname, and stories tell of performers in dire circumstances in effect mortgaging the cherished rāga they were best known for, agreeing not to perform it again until a debt was repaid. In the world of court patronage, improvisation served as a primary vehicle for male musicians to show their skills and to compete with opponents for musical and financial glory (For a colorful description of such a courtly contest, see Allen 1998:38–40.) Male performers typically did not rehearse or discuss the contents of a program in advance. They would meet on the stage platform a few minutes before a performance, something like a "pickup" group in jazz, ready to compete with each other to see who would come out on top.

The Hereditary Male Temple Service Musician. Hindu temples have long supported groups of ritual and artistic specialists, ranging from priests to female *dēvadāsis* and groups of male musicians. In Śiva temples, male singers called *ōduvārs* perform devotional *tēvāram* hymns (Peterson 1989). And a patriarchal social community with some kinship links to women of the *dēvadāsi* community has for centuries provided musicians for an instrumental temple ensemble known as the large or great ensemble, *periya mēḷam* (see the photograph on the book cover). The ensemble features the long double-reed aerophone *nāgasvaram* and double-headed membranophone *tavil*, supplemented by *śruti peṭṭi* drone box and small hand-held cymbals called *tāḷam*. Unlike the *dēvadāsis*, whose temple dedication was banned in 1947, the *periya mēḷam* tradition continues today inside and also outside of temples—for a range of domestic ritual observances and on the concert stage as well.

∞

Generation of auspiciousness by musicians and dancers. *In 1948, the year after India's independence and the banning of* dēvadāsi *dedication, prominent representatives of* periya mēḷam *and* dēvadāsi *families constituted themselves as a new legal-social entity under a new name,* Iśai Veḷḷāḷar, *"farmers of music" (Irschick 1986:215). In taking the name* Veḷḷāḷar, *they associated themselves with the respected* Śudra *agriculturalist caste of Tamiḻ Nāḍu and distanced themselves from derogatory caste names by which they had previously been called. Just as* dēvadāsis *had been uniquely qualified to perform auspicious dance and ritual activities for the deities of a temple and for the king, the male musicians of the* periya mēḷam *were, and remain today, specialists in* mangaḷa iśai, *auspicious music. Their music is considered absolutely essential for a variety of settings inside temples and outside, for example, at weddings (for which in the past* dēvadāsi *dance was also an essential component). At the moment in a wedding when the bridegroom ties the* tāli, *a thin cotton necklace, around the bride's neck, the* periya mēḷam *ensemble plays loudly so as to drown out and drive away inauspicious noises or forces.*

Periya mēḷam *music is today a vital marker of virtually all important ritual occasions, including opening and closing ceremonies of music festivals (although* nāgasvaram *performers are rarely given prime concert slots during the major festivals). To many South Indian Hindus, the sound of this music* means *temple. When Tamiḻ emigrants to Malaysia and Burma, where there were no Hindu temples, first heard* nāgasvaram *music over the radio in the late 1930s after decades living outside India, many reported that they felt they were* hearing *the Hindu temple, an intense emotional experience.*

∞

The context in which *nāgasvaram* performers have the opportunity to show their musicianship to the largest public is during annual temple festivals. Portable images of the deity are brought out of the temple and

FIGURE 4.4 *Temple car preparing to go in procession, Kumbakonam, 1969. (Courtesy of David Sanford)*

taken in *tērs,* large wooden-wheeled carts (Figure 4.4), through the streets around the temple, returning inside only at dawn. The musicians have expanses of time in which to develop their improvisations—imagine starting to play around nine o'clock in the evening with the knowledge that sometime around sunrise you might be getting close to ending your performance!

The "Emperor of Nāgasvaram": T. N. Rajarattinam Pillai. The outstanding *nāgasvaram* performer of the twentieth century and one of the greatest performers of Karṇāṭak music on any instrument was Tiruvavadudurai Natesa Rajarattinam Pillai (1898–1956). He was born into a family of musicians in a small village in Tañjāvūr District. His father, a *nāgasvaram* musician, died soon after his son's birth. Rajarattinam was adopted by his uncle, also an excellent *nāgasvaram* player, who died of cholera in 1903 at the age of only twenty-eight. Raised then by his maternal grandfather, Rajarattinam was given training in *nāgasvaram* from eminent members of his community and in vocal music from the respected Brahmin violinist Tirukkodikaval Krishnayyar. When he was about twelve years old, Rajarattinam was appointed as a *nāgasvaram* musician to a local religious monastery. His name spread as he gained a reputation for his flawless intonation, his ability to play *brikka* fast speed passages with great accuracy, and the depth of his musical imagination.

As his fame grew Rajarattinam used his influence to raise the status of *periya mēḷam* musicians. They did not suffer the same degree of social censure as *dēvadāsis* but were still perceived and treated as an inferior social group by the higher castes (Terada 2000). Rajarattinam made it a point of honor to perform only under the same conditions as Brahmin musicians. *Periya mēḷam* musicians had for generations performed barechested and standing. He was the first *nāgasvaram* musician to perform wearing a Western-style silk shirt instead of barechested. At the Tyagaraja festival in Tiruvaiyāṟu in 1939 Rajarattinam insisted that his group perform seated on the platform instead of standing. This was allowed after lengthy negotiation with the festival organizers. In processions during annual temple festivals, Rajarattinam began the practice of *periya mēḷam* musicians performing seated in an open truck rather than walking and performing standing (both practices are observed today).

"The Audience Would Not Be Satisfied If He Did Not Play This Rāga". *Nāgasvaram* players in the early twentieth century were appreciated above all for their skill at elaborating rāgas in lengthy *ālāpana*. As a mature artist this was Rajarattinam Pillai's special love. Of all the rāgas he performed he is remembered most for his performance of Tōḍi (Terada 1992:247). A scalar summary and some phrases of Tōḍi rāga are given in Activity 4.3 (CD track 19; also see CD track 24 for another example of Tōḍi). As you listen to the ornamented scale and then the phrases, write down your perceptions of which *svaras* take particular types of ornaments and which are rendered without ornament. Then, listen ahead to Rajarattinam's *ālāpana* in CD track 20—can you hear the phrases identified by Viswanathan occurring in the music of the

nāgasvaram? All in all, which *svaras* seem to fulfill important functions in Tōḍi? If you were writing a treatise on rāga, which would you designate as the "life-giving" *jīva svara* of Tōḍi?

ACTIVITY 4.3 *Scalar Summary and Phrases in Tōḍi Rāga* (CD Track 19)

Ārōhaṇa *(ascent)*

sa	ri	ga	ma	pa	dha	ni	$\overline{\text{sa}}$
C	D♭	E♭	F	G	A♭	B♭	C

Avarōhaṇa *(descent)*

$\overline{\text{sa}}$	ni	dha	pa	ma	ga	ri	sa
C	B♭	A♭	G	F	E♭	D♭	C

Some phrases at the beginning of Rajarattinam Pillai's ālāpana, *sung by T. Viswanathan (times refer to when phrases begin in CD track 19):*

1:00 sa sa ri ga , ma , pa pa pa ma ga
1:09 ni ni dha dha , ni $\overline{\text{sa}}$ $\overline{\text{ri}}$ $\overline{\text{sa}}$ $\overline{\text{sa}}$ $\overline{\text{sa}}$
1:17 sa ri ga ma dha ni $\overline{\text{ri}}$ $\overline{\text{ga}}$ $\overline{\text{ri}}$ ni dha ma ga ri ri
1:22 $\underline{\text{pa}}$ $\underline{\text{dha}}$ $\underline{\text{ni}}$ sa ri ga ma pa dha ni $\overline{\text{sa}}$ $\overline{\text{ri}}$ $\overline{\text{ga}}$
1:27 $\overline{\text{ga}}$ $\overline{\text{ma}}$, $\overline{\text{ga}}$ $\overline{\text{ri}}$ ni dha ma ga ri ri
1:32 ri ga ma dha ni $\overline{\text{ri}}$ $\overline{\text{ga}}$, $\overline{\text{ga}}$ $\overline{\text{ri}}$ ni dha ma ga ri ri
1:36 ga ma dha ni $\overline{\text{ri}}$ ni dha ma ga ri ri
1:38 ga ma ga , ri , sa

Ālāpana *in Tōḍi Rāga (CD Track 20).* Relatively early in his career, in 1934 Rajarattinam Pillai recorded a double-sided 78 RPM disk of *ālāpana* in Tōḍi rāga, playing only with drone accompaniment, without supporting *nāgasvaram* or *tavil* drum. Just as Nagarathnammal shortened her rendering of *Vaddani* to fit the three-minute 78 RPM format, Rajarattinam had to perform *ālāpana* for one of the most majestic Karṇāṭak rāgas in a tiny fraction of the time available in concert. In CD track 20, the second side of the double set, we begin listening at the halfway point of his recorded *ālāpana*. Having already introduced the low range of the rāga in the first side of the set, he is beginning to play fast passages throughout its entire range. His incredible control is evident—each *svara* is rendered clearly even at high rates of speed.

In the latter part of his career, Rajarattinam moved to concentrate more on musical lyricism than on speed, and he adopted a larger, lower-pitched *nāgasvaram* that gave his music a warmer, rich tone. Rajarattinam's style of playing was tremendously influential not just on other *nāgasvaram* performers but also on most all of the major Karṇāṭak vocalists and instrumentalists of his day—something akin to the revolutionary influence of Charlie Parker on jazz in the early days of bebop.

> Give me the microphone! The fall of pitch level and the rise of "crooning." *The lowering of pitch level by Rajarattinam was part of a general trend in the early mid-twentieth century, by instrumentalists and vocalists, to lower the* śruti, *pitch level, of performance. The average male and female singing pitch dropped as concerts began to be amplified. Stories abound of musicians in the days before the microphone whose high, powerful voices projected over formidable distances. With the advent of the microphone came a phenomenon disparagingly called "crooning" by its detractors—the singer huddled close to the microphone, using its power to amplify the sound rather than singing with a full head and chest voice.*

A NEW WORLD OF PERFORMANCE: CONCERT HALLS, MEDIA, AND AUDIENCES IN THE URBAN ENVIRONMENT

The *kriti*, which today forms the foundation of Karṇāṭak concerts, played a relatively small role in the world of court and temple male professional performance a century ago. What is now considered "traditional" in Karṇāṭak music performance is only just over a half century old. The new urban audience generated for music listening in the age of the public concert brought different aesthetics, standards, and desires to the concert hall than the royal or elite merchant patrons of old. Many of the new listeners had little knowledge of Karṇāṭak music and found the extended, intellectually challenging improvisations of the older generation of musicians impossibly esoteric. The new media of radio and recording demanded short, concise performances. And in the cities to which South Indians from small towns and villages were migrating en masse, rickshaw drivers, office workers, and high court judges alike had to be at work early in the morning. Performances lasting many hours were gradually replaced by shorter concerts containing a new "mix" in which compositions—with tuneful melodies and texts on which musical neophytes could focus—became much more central and improvisation was attenuated (Catlin 1985).

At the beginning of the twentieth century, music lovers in Chennai and other South Indian cities began to form organizations to sponsor public performances, called *sabhās*. These were the germ of what became by the 1930s a thriving network of concert halls. In 1927 an "All-India Music Conference" was organized in conjunction with the Indian National Congress party meeting at Chennai. The unexpected success and surplus proceeds of the conference led to the founding of the Music Academy of Madras, which became more than simply a *sabhā* by sponsoring not only concerts, but scholarly conferences and dance and music classes as well. By the early 1930s the Academy began holding its music conferences in the latter part of December each year, with morning academic sessions followed by afternoon and evening concerts. Today its conference is at the heart of the annual December "Music Season" and its *Journal* is the major scholarly publication on South Indian music.

The Development of Radio. In the burgeoning urban metropolis of Chennai, public concerts, gramophone recordings, and radio all evolved simultaneously, although influenced by different commercial and ideological forces. While commercial recording companies were almost wholly owned by European entrepreneurs, Indian businesspeople—many of them dedicated Congress party activists—quickly gained considerable influence over radio as it developed, using it both to advance the nationalist cause and to provide employment opportunities for musicians. The Madras Radio Club was founded in 1924. In its first days a speaker was set up along the oceanside Marina Beach in Chennai, a popular place for weekend promenades, and programs were broadcast on Sundays to the strolling weekenders. Madras Corporation Radio was formed in 1930, and soon phonograph records of popular artists were being broadcast to large crowds that would gather specifically to hear the music. In 1938 the Madras Corporation Radio was incorporated into the expanding national network, All India Radio. With India's independence in 1947, All India Radio quickly became a major force in musical patronage, hiring slates of musicians to become "staff artists" at each of its many stations around the country (see Neuman 1990:172–186 on All India Radio's patronage of North Indian musicians). Today stations around the country supply regular employment for hundreds of male and female staff artists, and major concert performers record broadcasts for the radio as well as for Doordarshan, the national government television network.

The Recording Industry: Commodification and Resistance. The overwhelming majority of early discs were by women *dēvadāsi* singers, whose sweet voices, recording companies found, sold more discs than male artists. The leading male musicians came to recording slowly and reluctantly. The revolutionary if de facto privileging of one fixed rendition of a song—mistakes and all—frozen on a 78 RPM disc, as "the" authoritative version, confronted Indian and non-Indian musicians alike with one of the most profound conceptual changes in the history of music (half a world away and at this exact moment, cultural theorist Walter Benjamin would pen his influential essay "The Work of Art in the Age of Mechanical Reproduction" [1935/2002]). For musicians who had been given their *guru's* repertoire during a long and arduous period of musical apprenticeship, this was their livelihood. A strong reason for their reluctance either to record or to broadcast their music was an intuitive apprehension that these unknown new technologies could reduce their direct control over the reception and consumption of their art—who could listen to it, under what circumstances, and what listeners could do with that music. Some were also opposed to recording because they felt that when people heard the recordings in the future, their style might be mocked as dated and old-fashioned, so pride as well as apprehension kept musicians away from the studios, despite exhortations for "masters of the art" to overcome their reluctance. Early voices of dissent notwithstanding, however, the recording industry grew and prospered in parallel fashion to radio, and by the 1940s almost all major concert artists, male and female, were recording on 78 RPM discs and multiple-disc sets.

"The Effect of the Performance Should Be Such As to Keep the Listeners Spell-Bound." The musician who best sensed the mood of the newly evolving listening public, and who is given credit for formulating a concert format that would appeal to that new public without losing sight of core musical values, was singer Ariyakkudi Ramanuja Ayyangar (1890–1967). Called simply "Ariyakkudi"—the name of his

family's ancestral village—by his many admirers, he came from a Brahmin family background. Ariyakkudi studied music in a disciplinary lineage of teachers and disciples leading directly back to Tyagaraja (Figure 4.5).

Tyagaraja (1767–1847)
  Manambuccavadi Venkata Subba Ayyar (cousin or nephew of Tyagaraja; nineteenth century)
    Pattanam Subramanya Ayyar (vocalist, composer; 1845–1902)
      Ramnad "Pucci" Srinivasa Ayyangar (vocalist, composer; 1860–1919)
        Ariyakkudi Ramanuja Ayyangar (vocalist; 1890–1967)

FIGURE 4.5 *Disciplinary lineage of Ariyakkudi Ramanuja Ayyangar (chronologically progressing left to right—teacher to student).*

Ariyakkudi's performance at the Tyagaraja festival in Tiruvaiyāṟu in 1918 was a major coming-out event for the talented young artist; by 1920 he was performing regularly around Chennai and was soon one of the most sought-after performers in South India. During his half-century performing career he received the highest honors in Karṇāṭak music, including in 1938 the title of *Saṅgīta Kalānidhi* ("crest jewel of music") from the Music Academy, the most coveted award to which a musician can aspire. His success was in no small measure due to a keen psychological sense of how to please an audience and an architect's eye for shaping performance, both clearly evident in a speech given probably in the late 1950s:

> A performer must be deeply conscious of his strengths and weaknesses. The effect of the performance should be such as to keep the listeners spell-bound, making them stay on to the very end, thirsting for still more. *Śruti* sense [a good sense of pitch], earnestness, a proper conception of *rāga-svarūpa* [rāga form], and good *laya-jñāna* [sense of timing]—without these, it is impossible to perform entertainingly.
>
> The concert should begin with a *varṇam* [etude-like piece] to be immediately followed by a few fast-tempo *kritis*. A short and crisp *ālāpana* of two or three of the rāgas of the *kritis* to be sung may be rendered. *Svara kalpana* must be limited and proportionate, and restricted to a few pieces, after a reasonable measure of *niraval*. The pieces selected should be of varied tāḷas, and no two of the same tāḷa need be sung consecutively. . . . The singer should enlist the cooperation of the accompanists all through with the object of making the concert a success. (Ramanuja Ayyangar 1990; text in brackets added)

The words peppering this passage—*immediately, fast, short, crisp, limited*—give a clear picture of the essence of his philosophy: Don't lose the listener! The improvisational forms that were the lifeblood of court competitions and are still central to all-night temple performances are here, but reduced to "short and crisp" *ālāpana*, "limited" *svara kalpana*, and "reasonable" *niraval*. To keep the audience's attention, Ariyakkudi left hardly any open spaces during a concert. When one song finished he immediately began the next, and within songs he left no pause at the conclusion of one section before starting into the next section. His focus was on keeping the concert moving. He found that a mixture of medium and fast tempo pieces elicited the best response from listeners. Ariyakkudi dramatically increased the number of compositions in a concert (Figure 4.6). He usually sang between five and seven *kritis* in the first part, then in "Part II" another half dozen or more miscellaneous shorter pieces, many of them dance music *jāvaḷis* and *padams* learned from women musicians.

Ariyakkudi's concerts lasted on average between three and four hours, and the format he evolved remains the organizational basis of most concerts today. While some concerts in Chennai are as brief as two and a half hours today (the length allotted for major recitals at the Music Academy), concerts presented by the South Indian community in

Varṇam, etude-like piece that warms up the voice
(8–10 minutes)

- Several *kritis* in medium and fast (contrasting) tempi, performed in alteration
  (3–5 *kritis*, total 30 minutes)
  - Main *kriti*, about an hour into the concert, with first (short) drum solo
    (30–45 minutes)
    - One or two very short *kritis*
      (5–10 minutes)
      - *Rāgam-tānam-pallavi*, with second (shorter) drum solo
        (30 minutes maximum)
        - *Part II:* miscellaneous shorter "light" pieces including *padams* and *jāvaḷis* from the dance repertoire
          (5–8 pieces, 45 minutes to 1 hour)

FIGURE 4.6 *The concert format of Ariyakkudi Ramanuja Ayyangar (progressing left to right through a performance).*

the United States and Europe tend to be longer, not infrequently three and a half or even four hours in duration.

Men Scripting and Singing Women's Inner Feelings. *Padams* and *jāvaḷis* are songs intended for interpretation by women in dance and giving voice to women's most intimate feelings and conversations. Yet almost all known composers of these songs were men, the majority of them Brahmin, some of them patrons or life-partners of particular *dēvadāsis*. Further complicating the gender history of these genres, while women often sing these intimate texts today, men often sang for women dancers in the past and, in the early days of the gramophone, recorded large numbers of *padams* and *jāvaḷis*. As part of his emphasis on presenting many compositions in concert, Ariyakkudi learned *padams* from co-author Viswanathan's grandmother Vina Dhanammal (1867–1938), the most highly respected woman musician of the early twentieth century (Figure 4.7). He also learned *padams* from one of his vocal students, Mylapore Gowri Ammal, a renowned *dēvadāsi* dancer dedicated to the

FIGURE 4.7 *Photograph showing Vina Dhanammal, the sole woman in the company of a group of eminent male musicians. Taken at the wedding of the daughter of Munuswamy Naidu (seated at left edge, in turban), secretary of a Chennai* sabhā, *1911.* *(Courtesy of T. Sankaran)*

Kapālīśvara temple in Chennai. In November 1932 the Odeon recording company released Ariyakkudi's recording of a Tamiḻ *padam* he had learned from Vina Dhanammal, "No Matter How Often I Tell You/ Ettanai connālum" (CD track 22). It is set in the magnificent rāga Sāvēri, one of the rāgas most closely associated with Dhanammal and her family tradition.

A scalar summary and some phrases of Sāvēri rāga as sung by T. Viswanathan are given in Activity 4.4 (CD track 21). Write down your perceptions of which *svaras* take particular types of ornaments in Sāvēri, which are rendered without ornament, also which *svaras* seem to be emphasized and to fulfill important functions.

ACTIVITY 4.4 *Scalar Summary and Phrases in Sāvēri Rāga* (CD Track 21)

Ārōhaṇa *(ascent)*

sa	ri	ma	pa	dha	s̄a
C	D♭	F	G	A♭	C

Avarōhaṇa *(descent)*

s̄a	ni	dha	pa	ma	ga	ri	sa
C	B	A♭	G	F	E	D♭	C

Phrases from the padam "No matter how often I tell you" (CD Track 22), sung by T. Viswanathan (times refer to when phrases begin in CD Track 21)

0:58 pa dha s̄a , s̄a ni r̄i s̄a ni dha
1:04 sa ri ma pa dha , r̄i , r̄i , r̄i s̄a ni dha pa ma ga , ri
1:13 sa ri ma pa dha ni dha pa ma ga , ri
1:18 pa ni dha pa dha ma pa dha
1:21 pa dha dha pa ma ga , ri
1:26 sa ri ma pa dha ni dha ma ga , , ri sa ri ga ri
1:33 sa ri ga ri ri , , ga ri sa n̲i̲ d̲h̲a̲
1:41 m̲a̲ d̲h̲a̲ ri , m̲a̲ d̲h̲a̲ ri , ri ma dha , dha pa ma ga , ri
1:51 sa ri pa ma dha pa dha ma ga ri
1:55 sa ri pa ma ga , ri , sa ri ga ri ri sa
2:01 sa , ri ga ri sa n̲i̲ d̲h̲a̲ p̲a̲ d̲h̲a̲ , sa

In singing "No Matter How Often I Tell You/Ettanai Connālum" (Activities 4.6 and 4.7) (CD track 22) Ariyakkudi voices the address of a mother to her wayward daughter. Even as she castigates the headstrong girl, the mother sees her own personality clearly reflected in the child's behavior and attitude. The song manifests a sharp wit, augmented by the use of colloquial Tamiḻ expressions such as, "Fighting is milk and fruit to you, girl!" (the third line of the *caraṇam*), which Ariyakkudi chooses to stress via repetition in this performance. In comparison to the performance of the *jāvaḷi* (CD track 18), where many lines of the brief text are repeated many times, the text of this *padam* is quite lengthy and dense, leaving Ariyakkudi accordingly much less time for repetition. A detailed listening guide for CD track 22 is available at http://www.wheatoncollege.edu/Faculty/MatthewAllen.html.

ACTIVITY 4.5 *Text and Translation of* "No Matter How Often I Tell You/*Ettanai Connālum*" *(CD Track 22)*
Composed by Vaidisvarankoil Subbarama Ayyar (ca. 1830–1880)
Rāga: Sāvēri; Tāḷa: ādi *(eight-beat cycle); Ariyakkudi Ramanuja Ayyangar, vocalist; violin and* mridaṅgam, *unknown*

Pallavi (begins at 0:03)	
Ettanai connālum teriyāda avar uḍan	No matter what I tell you, you don't understand me
Ēn piṇangi koḷvāy mahaḷē	Why do you continue this relationship (with him), my daughter?
Anupallavi (begins at 0:48)	
Attanai aḷitta kumarēcar vaittālum enna	The generous lord Kumaresar (Murugan, son of Śiva) who gives so much, even if he scolds you or ignores you, what of it?
Āttirap paḍuhiṟāy peṇ puttiyālē, anbuḷḷa pōdu kōbam irukkum men mēlē	You become distressed and angry because of your woman's mind; when

	someone loves you, it's also natural that he will sometimes get angry
Rāttiri rāmāyaṇam kēṭṭum appālē, rāmarukkuc cītai muṟai enna enbadu pōlē	After listening the whole night to the Rāmāyaṇa, you still ask, "What relation is Sītā to Rāma?" (i.e., you could listen to the Rāmāyaṇa all night and still not know how the hero and heroine are related to each other!) (No matter what I tell you . . .)
Caraṇam (begins at 1:49)	
Koṇḍavar nayattilum mayattilum colluvār	Your husband (Murugan) subtly weaves a web of illusion, saying to you,
Kōdaiyē pottukkoṇḍu pōnadu ennaḍi	"Oh girl, why do you feel so upset?" (What is the big deal? Why is this a surprise to you?)
Caṇḍai unakku pālum paḻamaḍi kuḍi kēḍi	Quarreling and fighting are just like milk and fruit to you, girl; you'll ruin our family!
Tāy pēr eḍuppāy vehu nērttiyāhavē tān	You'll take your mother's name just perfectly; you'll torture my name very well (the mother realizes that her daughter is hot-tempered and impetuous just like her)
Mīnaviḻiyāḷē unakkā inda tuḍukku, viralattanai uṇḍu ēn inda muḍukku	Oh beautiful fish-eyed girl, why this insolence? You're no bigger than a tiny little finger! Why this persistence?

Nān orutti idaṟkku ellām pōḍā viṭṭāl taḍukku, nānum oru peṇṇē enṟu nī kulukku vāy aḍakku	If a woman like me doesn't put a stop to all your foolishness (if I don't cover up your defects), you'll say "I'm also a lady!" strutting around and putting on airs. Shut your mouth! (No matter what I tell you . . .)

[Free translation from the Tamil̲ by T. Viswanathan and Matthew Allen]

A HEREDITARY MUSIC FAMILY

This final section examines the environment in which sisters T. Brinda and T. Muktha (Figure 4.2) grew up and learned music and their pivotal role in developing a new performance persona for women. They were born into a large and distinguished hereditary lineage of musicians and dancers tracing their ancestry to the city and court of Tañjāvūr, leading many in the family to prefix the initial T. to their given name (Figure 4.8).

When Brinda and Muktha were girls, the human focal point of the extended family was their grandmother, the unquestioned family matriarch Vina Dhanammal. A vocalist and performer on the stringed instrument *vīṇā*, Dhanammal achieved a level of respect from male musicians unparalleled by any other woman musician of her day, and her first recordings in 1932 (at age sixty-five) were heavily promoted (Figure 4.9). Dhanammal was renowned for her unmatched repertoire of *kritis* (especially those of Muttusvami Dikshitar), *padams*, and *jāvaḷis* and for her masterful, slow-speed style of rendering rāgas. Most major musicians and dedicated connoisseurs in South India made the pilgrimage more than once to the Friday evening music sessions at her house in Ramakrishnan Street in the Georgetown section of Chennai, where "pin-drop silence" ruled as she would play for friends and acquaintances who would gather.

FIGURE 4.8 *Photograph of Vina Dhanammal and family, 1936. Bottom row, left to right: T. Viswanathan, S. Bhagyalakshmi, T. Ranganathan, S. Kalpakambal, S. Vasudevan. Second row: T. Brinda, T. Kamakshi, T. Lakshmiratnam, Vina Dhanammal, T. Rajalakshmi, T. Jayammal, T. Muktha. Third row: T. Kothandaraman, Srinivasan, T. Soundararajan, S. Minakshi, T. Balasarasvati, T. Abhiramasundari, T. Sankaran, T. Vijayakrishnan. Fourth row: T. Govardhanan, S. Sivaraman, T. Varadan.* *(Photograph by G. K. Vale. Courtesy of Jody Cormack Viswanathan)*

A Dual Musical Enculturation and Education. The young women seated at opposite ends of the second row in Figure 4.8 were pioneers. Together with a handful of other women including M. S. Subbulakshmi (b. 1916), D. K. Pattammal (b. 1919), and M. L. Vasanthakumari (1928–1990), T. Brinda and T. Muktha would lead the way for women to begin performing in the new concert format (Figure 4.6), which combined compositions with a variety of improvisational genres previously only performed by men. Their education involved both the absorption of their own family tradition—from their mother Kamakshi, aunts, and grandmother Dhanammal—and a period of rigorous training with a male *guru* from outside the family. As young girls Brinda and Muktha were sent to study with and live in the family of the master musician Kancipuram Nayana Pillai (1889–1934), renowned for his huge repertoire of

A HEART-MELTING INSTRUMENT!

Dr. RAMA RAO REGRETS THE DECLINE
OF THE VEENA

"India was slowly giving up the Veena, a heart-melting musical instrument, in favour of the Harmonium, a change from Heaven to Hell" remarked Rao Saheb Dr. U. Rama Rao at a Veena Performance.

(Extract from the "Hindu" dated the 6th December, 1932.)

"Columbia"

HAVE PRESERVED FOR ALL TIME THE MUSIC OF THE GREATEST VEENA PLAYER IN INDIA:–

VEENA DHANAM

REAL TIME-HONOURED CARNATIC MUSIC WONDERFULLY RENDERED FOR FUTURE GENERATIONS.

A unique opportunity for students of the Veena to learn from a master musician.

VEENA DHANAM'S FIRST RECORD IS NOW AVAILABLE FROM ALL COLUMBIA DEALERS **Rs. 3-8** each.

SOLE DISTRIBUTORS:

ORR'S COLUMBIA HOUSE

MOUNT ROAD MADRAS

FIGURE 4.9 *Newspaper advertisement for Vina Dhanammal's first recordings.* The Hindu, *Chennai, December 16, 1932.* *(Courtesy of Matthew Allen)*

Tyagaraja's *kritis,* his skills at singing *rāgam-tānam-pallavi,* and his arrangements of the fifteenth-century composer Arunagirinadar's *tiruppuhal* hymns, a genre of compositions set to long and complex tāḷa cycles.

Like Ariyakkudi, Nayana Pillai was one of the early male musicians to add more *kritis* into his concerts. He attached extensive improvisation, especially *svara kalpana,* to his performance of *kritis,* and was renowned for his mastery of the rhythmic aspects of music. For rhythmic accompaniment he typically had seven percussionists, a phenomenon unique in South India and known as the "full bench." Nayana Pillai regularly stumped this august assembly by playing *svara kalpana* improvisations that they were incapable of following and by springing on them his settings of *tiruppuhal* hymns in complex rhythmic cycles (for example, the hymn *kādi mōdi* is set to twenty-one beats, divided 3 + 3 + 5 + 2 + 4 + 4). The criticism his concerts received for being too rhythmically oriented was felt in his family to be motivated by jealousy (and fear!) because few musicians—drummers or otherwise—could challenge his rhythmic expertise.

It was therefore not just to any teacher that their mother Kamakshi sent Brinda and Muktha for training. She chose for them a *guru* legendary for what was at the time a quintessentially *male* form of music making—about as different from their family style as could be. Nayana Pillai was extremely proud of his young students and decided, flying in the face of prejudices and stereotypes of the day, that they were capable of doing anything a male musician was. He found in the elder sister Brinda in particular the perfect vehicle to combat what he saw as many of his colleagues' pervasive *āṇ garvam,* "male arrogance."

"I Am Going to Snub These Male Chauvinists." The following passages are taken from interviews conducted by co-author Allen with Dhanammal's grandson T. Sankaran (Figure 4.10). A capable singer who never trained formally with a teacher, Sankaran eschewed music performance as a profession, but his two primary careers, as director of All India Radio stations throughout India (1938–61) and director of the *Tamil Isai Sangam* Music School in Chennai (1961–85), involved extensive daily contact with musicians. He was a deep repository of Karṇāṭak music history, with a generous spirit, sharp wit, and acute powers of observation. He knew all the major musicians of South India and counted among his friends many Hindustāni musicians as well. He published dozens of articles and a book of Tamil biographies of South Indian musicians and served as a consultant for many South Indian and foreign scholars during his "long innings," as he would put it. Sankaran passed away in January 2001 at the age of ninety-five.

FIGURE 4.10 *T. Sankaran.* *(Courtesy of Jody Cormack Viswanathan)*

His concert was called the full bench. There'll be nine people on stage. And to manage this many people, his sense of rhythm must be . . . he must be very clear-headed. [M. A.—And all these percussionists, they must have rehearsed together a lot?] No no no: no rehearsal! It's a competition—how could it be rehearsed? This is not a situation for rehearsal. Because, otherwise, how can he shine in a competitive setup? Nine people. It was called the full bench. It was called the *nava grahas* [nine planets].

He saw in Brinda and Muktha a chance to snub the male chauvinism. See, in those days only the men sang *svara kalpana* and *rāgam-tānam-pallavi*, never females. Girls were never *taught* those things, in the first place. But this Brinda's sense of rhythm and receptivity was something remarkable. And then, it was difficult to approach our grandmother Dhanammal for lessons. She'll just snub you. So my aunt took these girls to Nayana Pillai. When he heard about it, Bhairavam Pillai the *mridaṅgam* player headed a delegation to Nayana Pillai's home to urge him to give up teaching the girls. "They are *already* Dhanammal's granddaughters. It's . . . fire! You want to add a storm into that? This is like fanning the fire with a hurricane! *Please* don't teach them." He and other like-minded gentlemen were afraid of fostering competition between the sexes. But Nayana Pillai turned a deaf ear to his pleas. He said, "No no no, we are one family. They have come. They are certainly not starving for music, but they have come to me. I must teach them." And he said, "I am going to snub these male chauvinists. I'll get these girls to sing everything."

And at another time, Abdul Karim Khan was here in the South; he was a great Hindustāni musician. He had *absolute* contempt for Karṇāṭak musicians. He will say, "You don't have any sense of *śruti* [pitch, intonation]." When Nayana Pillai and Govindaswami Pillai [violinist and close friend of Nayana Pillai] and all these people went to listen to him, he unleashed a *tirade* about these Karṇāṭak musicians. "You fellows have no *śruti*, you cannot. . . ." Govindaswami Pillai couldn't speak—his eyes got bloodshot. Nayana Pillai had taken Brinda with him; she was just a teenager. He whispered to Govindaswami Pillai, "He is challenging us. Let him face this girl, who will just take up the challenge." He said to Abdul Karim Khan, "Alright. You sing whatever you want." And Brinda sang *svaram* for everything Abdul Karim Khan initiated. Whatever he did, she transcribed in *svaram* [i.e., she imitated his *ālāpana* perfectly, voicing the correct solfège names of the *svaras* as she sang]. That put the lid on that fellow. He got snubbed.

That's how Brinda loved to sing *svaram*, which was never allowed by my grandmother. She would never encourage ladies to sing like that. She thought it was unwomanly, to just beat your thigh like that [slaps his thigh] and sing. She always insisted on women strumming the *tambūra* and singing. Nayana Pillai taught Brinda to sing everything, but before he could complete it he died. (T. Sankaran, personal communication, December 31, 1987, and January 5 and 13, 1988; text in brackets added)

Music and Gender Today. Brinda and Muktha, together with a handful of other women, began performing full concerts including every kind of improvisation and received many awards during their career as a duo and subsequently as solo artists, Brinda eventually receiving the Music Academy's highest honor, *Saṅgīta Kalānidhi*. Today it is no longer a shock or even a novelty to see a woman leading a group on stage, although attitudes expressed by some male musicians and critics are still sometimes ambivalent towards women's capabilities.

On the one hand, concerts by women artists are at least as numerous as those by male artists today, women students far outnumber men in the numerous music colleges, and there seems to be continuing consensus that women have more attractive voices than do men. The story of one early twentieth-century private *sabhā* run by Tirumalayya Naidu, who spent the then-princely sum of twenty-five *rupees* every month for concerts by "ladies only" at his house, was recounted by T. Sankaran: "I have attended one or two when I was about ten or twelve years of age. His dictum was: 'Even if it is for braying, it should be by a she ass, never a jack ass'" (personal communication, December 10, 1991).

On the other hand, some male accompanists still avoid playing for women, even the top female artists. There is a lingering perception in some circles that women are not as well equipped to handle the intellectual or mathematical aspects of music as are men. T. Sankaran characterized the following attitude as "tardily dying" as of 1988: "The males used to say, 'Who is this woman? She simply sings . . . she has got a beautiful voice; she is trying to boss over us. She is just a parrot, learning a few songs and repeating them'" (personal communication, January 5, 1988).

SUMMARY: AN ANCIENT AND MODERN TRADITION OF MUSICAL-SOCIAL BEHAVIOR

This chapter has presented a social and historical context for the understanding of contemporary Karṇāṭak performance, in the process implicitly developing two notions that may now be stated explicitly: "Tradition" can be simultaneously ancient and thoroughly modern, and music is constantly in interaction with the society in which it lives.

Chapter 2 illustrated, among other things, the antiquity of the discourse on Karṇāṭak music—the fact, for example, that rāga has been discussed, debated, and treasured in India since at least the ninth century A.D. The discussion of *Kaligiyuṇṭē* in Chapter 3 demonstrated how in South India today, composed music can be quite flexible and improvised music quite structured. This chapter has shown how the balance between these elements has changed in the last century. Karṇāṭak music, far from being a "timeless" static unchanging system, has developed through specific social and historical circumstances, shaking off old attributes and taking on new ones at every stage of its growth. No matter how fixed it may seem at first glance, like so many other traditions, Karṇāṭak music is always evolving in response to musicians' creativity and to changes in society.

Karṇāṭak music today is perceived as an elite art music tradition, both by the relatively small portion of the population that is its core audience and the much larger public whose preferred listening music is that of the cinema and "Bollywood" (see Chapter 5). How did this come to be? To arrive at an understanding of contemporary Karṇāṭak music, the histories and perspectives of a group of musicians and social commentators, diverse in terms of gender and social class, were profiled in this chapter. The lives of these individuals illustrate how developments in musical repertoire, style, and thinking are nested within social and historical forces and processes. Musical developments reflect, but also affect, these forces. South Indian music and dance performers played important roles in both local and national cultural politics in the twentieth century, together with the scholars and critics who developed and disseminated a discourse that sees Karṇāṭak music and *bharata nāṭyam* dance as South India's great "classical" arts (Allen 1998:22–52). As these forms left the courts and temples to become concert arts comparable in their presentation to European classical music or ballet, they came to play a role on the national stage—*bharata nāṭyam* in particular, seen by many Indians as the country's "national" dance—in the Indian independence movement, and then in the nation-building project of "integration" that followed.

CHAPTER 5

Regional and Modern Traditions: Contemporary Music Making in South India and Beyond

MUSIC IN KĒRAḶA

This final chapter moves beyond Tamiḻ Nāḍu to other states of South India and abroad and beyond the "classical" tradition to the worlds of regional folk, popular cinema, and "fusion" music. Four case studies of contemporary music making, historically rooted yet constantly dynamic and outward-looking, collectively suggest paths South Indian music may be taking into the future.

The southwestern state of Kēraḷa faces out across the Arabian Sea toward the Middle East and Africa. Its geographical situation has been one factor in making Kēraḷa an extremely heterogeneous environment (Groesbeck and Palackal, in Arnold 2000:929–951). Approximately fifty-eight percent of its people are Hindu. Twenty-three percent are Muslim, a distinctive community called *Māppilas*, including descendants of Arab immigrants and converts from Hinduism. Nineteen percent of the state's population is Christian, a community dating to the fifth century A.D. that has accommodated successive influences from Syrian Christian to Roman Catholic and, since the nineteenth century, Protestant sects. From as early as the fourth century A.D. the area around Cochin has had an important Jewish population, although the number of residents is today less than one hundred since the emigration of most of the remaining community after the foundation of the state of Israel in 1948. The original language of the region was an archaic form of Tamiḻ; Malayāḷam emerged as a distinct language around the tenth century A.D. The state has the highest literacy rate in India, over ninety percent.

FIGURE 5.1 Iḍakka *drummer Satheesan of Peruvanam village.* *(Courtesy of Parvathy Hadley)*

Iḍakka, a Pressure Drum from Kēraḷa (CD Track 23). One distinct feature of the Kēraḷa soundscape is a wide variety of percussion instruments and drumming traditions. The small tension drum *iḍakka* (Figure 5.1) is similar in its construction and tonal capabilities to West African talking drums. *Iḍakka* is used to accompany a number of Kēraḷa musical genres, including *tyāṇi*, prayer songs sung beside the steps leading into the inner sanctum during temple *pūjas* (CD track 23), and the dance drama form *Kathakaḷi*, literally, "story-play" (CD track 24). The drummer plays it with a curved, very thin stick in the right hand and holds the drum by the ropes connecting the drum heads with the left.

Squeezing these ropes changes the pitch of the drum, and a "rolling hand" technique is used to play consecutive very quick strokes with the stick. In the hands of a fine performer the instrument can play complete melodies—some Marars, a Kēraḷa temple drummer-singer caste, are renowned for their ability to play *kritis* on *iḍakka*. Liner notes to the 1961 recording on which CD track 23 was originally included provide no details on the performance. Two senior scholars of Kēraḷa music, L.S. Rajagopalan and Viswanath Kaladharan, who listened to the recording at our request, reported that it is a portion of a song from the temple vocal repertoire, a *tyāṇi* or perhaps an *aṣṭapaḍi* from Jayadeva's *Gītagōvinda*. Typically, after a vocalist sings a verse, the *iḍakka* player responds on the drum. In CD track 23, P. M. Narayana Marar plays one verse from a song and then a short *kalaśam*, a rhythmic flourish that serves as a concluding pattern.

Kathakaḷi *Dance Drama.* Every state of South India has its own forms of dance drama, combining music, dance, and acting. *Kathakaḷi* is one of the most well known partly because of the dramatic and distinctive costumes and facial makeup worn by its performers. *Kathakaḷi* is traditionally performed only by men and grew directly out of a martial environment under the patronage of Nambūdiri Brahmins, Kṣatriyas, and petty chieftains from the Nāyar caste in the seventeenth century. Lower-ranking Nāyars served these chieftains as retainers and warriors. Their boys were trained in military arts from a young age in small gymnasiums called *kaḷari*. Training took place during the heavy monsoon season, when the muscles were most flexible and when neither agriculture nor war could be practiced. Nāyar soldiers were recruited into the first *Kathakaḷi* dramas; its actors trained in the same gymnasiums as young warriors, using many of the same techniques.

The plays of a ruling prince, Kottayam Tampuran (ca. 1645–1716), were the first to be called *Kathakaḷi*; the term *katha*, story, implied the wide range of deities and epic heroes he wrote about—not just Rāma or Kṛṣṇa, as was customary in earlier dance drama. In earlier dance dramas the actors spoke and sang, but in *Kathakaḷi* these functions are separated. A pair of vocalists articulates the text, leaving the actors free to concentrate on their vigorous *tāṇḍava* dancing and mimetic portrayal. This separation of functions contributed to the developing ethos of abstract nonrepresentation in *Kathakaḷi*, so beautifully embodied in the fantastic costumes and makeup of the characters (Figures 5.2 and 5.3; see also Zarrilli 2000 and Jones 1970).

FIGURE 5.2 Kathakaḷi *actors portraying King Nala and* hamsa *(the swan). From the play* Naḷa Caritam. *(Courtesy of Jan Steward)*

Character Types, Costume, and Makeup. The characters are grouped by facial makeup types, ranging on a spectrum from refined to coarse, reminiscent of the aesthetics of the Javanese *wayang kulit* puppet theater. Color symbolism is extremely important. *Pacca,* "green," characters are the most refined, morally upright heroes, kings, and deities, such as Rāma. Their refined nature is indicated both by the makeup and by their actions on stage, always self-possessed, in control, never uttering a sound. *Minukku,* "shining," characters are women or Brahmins of high spiritual qualities; this is the only category whose makeup and costumes are close to real life. The *katti,* "knife," characters have some redeeming qualities; their makeup base is green, although red moustaches and red patterns above the eyes indicate a meaner, coarser nature. *Tāḍi,* "beard," characters are of three types, the white beard being relatively the most virtuous, the red beard evil, and the black beard equally evil and also scheming. Finally, the *kari,* "black," class is reserved for female demons, often wearing comic false breasts, their jet-black faces covered with red and white dots. The coarser characters, while not talking, often utter cries and grunts as befit their unrefined nature (Zarrilli 1990:331–336).

Most characters have thick lower-body skirts, elaborate crowns, and facial makeup that includes the *cuṭṭi*, a white paper border framing the face from ear to ear. There are very few props on stage. Most objects are suggested through *mudrās*, the mimetic gestures of the actors. The most important stage property is a multicolored curtain held up by assistants, behind which characters stand before emerging onto stage. Waiting behind the curtain, their headdresses are usually visible, giving the audience a foretaste of the next part of the story.

FIGURE 5.3 Kathakaḷi actors portraying the five Pāṇḍava brothers from the epic Mahābhārata. *(Courtesy of Jan Steward)*

Changes in the Twentieth Century. During the late nineteenth and early twentieth centuries, the same societal pressures that affected musicians and dancers in Tami<u>l</u> Nāḍu came to bear upon the arts in Kēraḷa. Young people educated in the British Victorian model came to see *Kathakaḷi* as just a "dumb show," and several of Kēraḷa's rulers in the late nineteenth century patronized European music and drama rather than their own. The all-night performances in temple courtyards or the courtyards of patrons' houses during the hot dry season became much briefer, following the same trajectory as performance in Tami<u>l</u> Nāḍu. In 1930, at almost exactly the same time that the Music Academy was founded in Chennai to support Karṇāṭak music, the great Malayāḷam poet Vallathol Narayana Menon (1878–1958) founded the Kēraḷa Kalāmaṇḍalam near the town of Thrissur (Trichur). Vallathol conceived of the Kalāmaṇḍalam as an institute that would compensate for the disappearance of traditional forms of patronage by training young people in *Kathakaḷi* and other traditional arts of Kēraḷa. The Kalāmaṇḍalam has been a major force in the reinvigoration of *Kathakaḷi* in Kēraḷa, in other parts of India, and on the international stage (Zarrilli 2000).

The Kathakaḷi *Music Ensemble.* A *Kathakaḷi* group includes vocalists and percussionists who typically stand throughout a performance. There are no melodic instruments. The *ponnāni*, "major musician," sings while keeping rhythm on a *cēṅṅilam*, a metal gong beaten with a short stick. The *śinkiḍi*, "minor partner," who sings sometimes in response to and sometimes together with the lead vocalist, plays *ilattāḷam*, a pair of small cymbals. The gong and cymbals carry the primary tāḷa-keeping function. There are three important drums in the ensemble. The double-headed *maddaḷam* accompanies all situations and characters. It is held horizontally across the player's thighs with a cloth wrapped around the waist and is played with both hands. The *ceṇḍa* is a cylindrical double-headed drum held vertically, played with two curved sticks. *Ceṇḍa* accompanies all male characters and can make a wide variety of expressive sounds. The *iḍakka*, which today usually only accompanies the *minukku* female characters (there is evidence that it accompanied male characters in the past, as on CD track 24), completes the ensemble. The drummers' primary function is less keeping tāḷa than reinforcing the movements and gestures of the actors. Figure 5.4, taken at a function in honor of *ceṇḍa* drummer Peruvanam Kuttan Marar (just right of center), contains the instruments of the *Kathakaḷi* ensemble as well as others.

FIGURE 5.4 *Photograph of the Rhythms Divine ensemble, September 2001. From left to right:* cēṅṅilam, kurum kuḻal, ilattāḷam, ceṇḍa, iḍakka, ceṇḍa *(Kuttan Marar),* timila, maddaḷam, kombu, conch. *(Courtesy of Parvathy Hadley)*

Kathakaḷi *Songs:* Ślōkam *and* Padam. *Ślōkams* are the narrative sections of the play set in the third person; they open scenes and prepare the audience for the dialogue portions that follow in *padams*. The *ślōkam* is a Sanskrit metrical verse set in a rāga but not to a tāḷa; this gives a singer great rhythmic freedom of interpretation. About eighty percent of *ślōkams* are sung without actors on stage. When an actor performs to a *ślōkam,* his gestures are kept relatively simple, the goal being to embody the mood described in the narrative.

The *Kathakaḷi padam* is set both in rāga and tāḷa. *Padams* carry the first-person dialogue of the play, are composed in a mixture of the Malayāḷam and Sanskrit languages, and occupy the majority of a play's duration. Like *kritis,* they usually have a *pallavi-anupallavi-caraṇam* structure, although *anupallavi* can be omitted and there is usually more than one *caraṇam.* The *padam* is danced by an actor who illustrates through mimed gestures the story narrated by the singers. Each line of a song is danced at least twice. The first time through, the actor establishes the subtext—the primary emotional mood of the line. For repetition(s) of the line, he "speaks" each word using gesture language.

Performance of Padam *from* Naḷa Caritam *(CD track 24).* CD track 24 contains part of the *caraṇam* section of a *padam* from the play *Naḷa Caritam*, the "story" or "conduct" of King Nala, written by Unnayi Variyar (ca. 1675–1716) and based on a subsidiary story from the *Mahābhārata*. Variyar developed the complex psychological state of the hero's mind with great refinement and sensitivity, making *Naḷa Caritam* one of the most loved *Kathakaḷi* plays. It is divided into four parts, traditionally performed on successive evenings. This *padam*, set in the third scene on the first evening, enacts the meeting of King Nala of Nishada with a golden *hamsa*, swan (see Figure 5.2). He comes upon the sleeping swan and, entranced, touches it. When the swan awakes with a cry, he apologizes for startling it. The swan then tells Nala about the great qualities of the beautiful princess Damayanti and offers to go as a messenger to her on his behalf (reminiscent of one role played by the *sakhī*, confidante, as discussed in Chapter 4). Nala and Damayanti eventually meet and, after overcoming obstacles placed in their path by a group of gods, are married, bringing to a close the first evening's performance.

The two vocalists sing while keeping the eight-beat *cempaṭa* tāḷa on the gong and cymbals. Of the drums heard on this recording, the high-pitched *ceṇḍa* is prominent, and the *maddaḷam* is present but less audible. The *iḍakka*, used today almost exclusively for female characters, can be heard briefly in the middle of the excerpt. As there are no female characters in this scene, the recording (made ca. 1961) provides evidence that in the recent past *iḍakka* has been used to accompany male characters as well (L. S. Rajagopalan and Rolf Groesbeck, personal communication 2002).

In the portion of the *padam* translated in Activity 5.1, Nala is delighted to have met someone who may help him win Damayanti, the princess. After this scene, the swan flies to Damayanti's garden, where it finds the princess and her maids dancing (Dominique Vitalyos, personal communication, 2002).

ACTIVITY 5.1 *Text and Translation of* Caraṇam *Section,* Kathakaḷi Padam *from* Naḷa Caritam
Composed by Unnayi Variyar (ca. 1675–1716); translated from the Malayāḷam by Dominique Vitalyos

Rāga: Tōḍi; Tāḷa: cempaṭa *(eight-beat cycle); M. E. P. Pillai and Gopinathan Nayar, vocalists; K. Damodaran Pannikar and Vasudeva Poduwal, drummers*

Palarum collikeṭṭu – naḷinamukhitan katha	Having heard about – the girl with the lotus face
Balavat angajārtti – perutittu hṛdi me	Pangs of love – grew in my heart
Oruvan sahāyamillenu – (urutaravedanayā maruvunna neram . . .	Thinking I was alone, with no one to help – (when I was in great pain . . .
Ninṟe paricayam vannu daivāl).	By the grace of god, I befriended you).

Note: Hyphens indicate pauses in middle of text lines; section of text in parentheses occurs after recording fades out.

This *padam* is set to Tōḍi rāga—already heard in CD tracks 19 and 20—and to *cempaṭa* tāḷa, an eight-beat cycle analogous to *ādi* tāḷa in Karṇāṭak music. The text lines begin at the same place in the tāḷa cycle as in Tyagaraja's *kriti Kaligiyuṇṭē* (CD track 14), three quarters of a beat after the first beat of the cycle. Recite the first phrase of the text while keeping tāḷa (Activity 5.2). Notice the syncopation of the text setting in the third and fourth beats in particular and the flexibility with which the singers phrase the line. Notice also how the vocalists sing the first half of each line at least twice, before singing the full line. A detailed listening guide for CD track 24 is available at http://www.wheatoncollege.edu/Faculty/MatthewAllen.html.

ACTIVITY 5.2 *Approximate Rhythmic Placement of Beginning of* Caraṇam *Text, over First Four Beats of* Cempaṭa *Tāḷa (CD Track 24)*

1 , , , 2 , , , 3 , , , 4 , , , 5 , , ,
pa la rum *col li keṭ ṭu* (continues . . .)

MUSIC OF THE CINEMA IN SOUTH INDIA

> While in many other parts of the world, changes in musical taste effect the kind of music used in films, here the situation is exactly the reverse. It is film music which sets trends and moulds musical tastes. The cultural niche occupied by pop music in the West is the preserve of Indian film music. (Baskaran 1996:54)

The film industry in India is staggering in its scope. Each year the studios of "Bollywood" (a nickname for the film industry in Bombay/Mumbai), Chennai, and Kolkata produce many more movies than are made in the United States. These are avidly consumed by South Asians at home and around the world and by millions of non–South Asians as well. While not all Indian movies contain as many songs—fifty—as the first South Indian "talkie" *Kalidas* (1931), it is rare to find an Indian movie without at least a dozen or more lavishly staged song-and-dance numbers. Major music directors today are often given star billing and are an integral part of the planning process of big budget movies, along with producers and directors.

The "Company Drama" and the Silent Cinema. The first South Indian silent film was made in 1912. At that time traveling drama companies provided a popular form of entertainment, cutting across caste and economic boundaries. The repertoire of these "company dramas," so called because they were run on commercial lines with professional actors, was limited to a relatively small set of mythological stories. These were presented as musicals; all actors had to be able to sing, and most danced as well. South Indian company drama songs were based on Karṇāṭak music and were augmented with significant North Indian influences because of the groups' contact with traveling Marāṭhī and Parsi language drama companies. Because of the importance of songs, the company drama format could not be appropriated by the silent cinema, but it did eventually serve as the model for early sound films. Silent cinema directors depended instead on actors like "Battling Mani" and "Stunt Raju" to attract an audience without a soundtrack:

> Silent cinema, when it was produced in Madras, did not affect the company dramas; both were able to coexist without any conflict. In the absence of sound, silent cinema in South India specialized in stunt sequences; it needed men who could impress the viewers by jumping from tall buildings. So the singers and musicians stayed on with the drama companies where they were assured of a steadier income than in the spasmodic production of silent movies. (Baskaran 1996:41)

Early Sound Films: The "Mythological." The directors of early sound movies turned to the company drama stage tradition for their subject matter. With their meager resources, they could not compete with the sophisticated stunts and technical effects in the American movies that were beginning to flood the Indian market by the 1930s. But they had at hand a ready stock of mythological subjects that had proved successful in filling houses for the drama companies. Actors, directors, songwriters, and musicians from the stage moved over to the new cinema studios en masse, with the result that the early sound films were essentially company drama productions, shot by a static camera. Until the first sound studios were opened in Chennai in the mid-1930s, films had to be made in North Indian studios:

> As these drama troupes who traveled to Bombay or Calcutta to make a film were operating in a new region and therefore had to bear the boarding and lodging expenses for the whole troupe, the tendency was to rush through and complete the project as quickly as possible. . . . Not much importance was given to continuity or appropriateness. In *Kōvalan* (1933), a film set somewhere between the third and fifth century A.D., one of the characters appears in a few scenes wearing spectacles. In *The Exile of Sītā (Sītā Vanavāsam,* 1934), Rāma opens an envelope with a postage stamp and postmarks on it. (Baskaran 1996:13)

As discussed in Chapter 4, during the early 1930s gramophone recordings and radio became a major presence in South India. The recording companies quickly joined forces with cinema companies, producing sets of 78 RPM recordings of songs from newly released movies. Prominent Karṇāṭak musicians who had been reluctant to record or broadcast their music were gradually lured into the new medium by the substantial financial incentives and the growing respectability that followed in the wake of those incentives.

The "Social." By the mid-1930s, contemporary sociopolitical issues began to make their way into the cinema, resulting in a new genre, the "social," which gradually displaced the "mythological" as staple movie fare. The first South Indian movie on a contemporary social theme, *Kausalyā* (1935), was a thriller "with a pistol-wielding woman as the chief protagonist" (Baskaran 1996:14). By 1937, many films advanced a strong nationalist sentiment and criticized economic and social inequities prevalent in Indian society. H. M. Reddy's Telugu film *Rythubidda* (1939) addressed the exploitation of workers by rapacious landlords, promoted Gandhian ideals, and satirized Westernization, bringing new respect to the Telugu cinema and attracting much negative attention from the British-controlled film censor board. Two years later, K. Subrahmanyam's Tamiḻ film *Thyāgabhūmi/Land of Sacrifice* propagandized in favor of Gandhi's most important programs: *svarāj* ("self-rule"), temple entry (the right of people of all castes to enter Hindu temples), anti-untouchability, temperance, and the rejection of imported garments in favor of *khādi* handspun and handwoven clothing. Its statements against the inequities of the caste system were particularly notable because practically the entire production team for the movie was Brahmin.

After India's independence the emphasis on contemporary social issues continued in South Indian film, but the focus shifted from nationalism to regional cultural and linguistic pride, especially in the state of Tamiḻ Nāḍu where, as discussed in Chapter 1, the movement to promote indigenous culture and music was particularly strong. A symbiotic link between politics and the cinema developed as politicians saw the potential of the medium for spreading their messages. While prominent politicians have emerged from the cinema in other South Indian states, the situation in Tamiḻ Nāḍu is particularly striking: Since 1967, all five Chief Ministers of the state have had strong associations with the cinema, two as dialogue writers and three as film stars.

The Playback Singer. Once technology made it possible for audio to be recorded independently of video, acting could be separated from singing, and the "playback" singer was born. Ethnomusicologist Alison Arnold explains: "Professional singers record the songs, which are then inserted into a film sound track and matched to the frames showing the actors mouthing the lyrics. At the film shooting, the song recording is played back through loudspeakers to ensure correct timing by the screen artist, hence the term *playback*" (Arnold 2000:538). In South India the eminent female vocalist D. K. Pattammal became the first to record a dubbed voiceover in the 1940 biographical film *Mahatma Gandhi*. The playback singer rapidly became an institution in Indian cinema and by the 1950s had completely replaced actor-singers (Greene, in Arnold 2000:542–546).

The Cinema and Karṇāṭak Music: A Parting of Ways. Karṇāṭak musicians were very active in the film world during the decade leading up to independence, but cinema music and Karṇāṭak music began to part ways by the early 1950s. Cinema music directors turned from art music toward the myriad regional Indian folk music traditions that were readily accessible to the mass audience. Their ears also tuned in to attractive sounds coming over the transom from overseas: Over the next several decades an eclectic mix of Hawaiian guitars, congas and bongos, salsa, lambada, funk, and rap joined indigenous Indian sounds to become an integral part of the cinema music soundscape.

Film music's movement away from a classical music sensibility alienated Karṇāṭak music performers and connoisseurs, and today cinema music and Karṇāṭak music proceed largely along separate parallel tracks, with a few exceptions. Karṇāṭak vocalist Madurai G. S. Mani's lecture-demonstrations illustrating rāgas through cinema songs draw large and enthusiastic audiences, and some musicians have argued that a dialogue between the two camps is an essential ingredient in ensuring the survival of Karṇāṭak music (Viswanathan 1989). Important contemporary South Indian music directors whose film soundtracks are readily available on CD and video are Ilaiyaraja, A. R. Rahman, and Vijaya Anand (see the Resources).

"When I Say Come/*Ba Ennalu*" (CD Track 25). Jude Matthew was born to Roman Catholic parents in Chennai in 1952. At age seven he fell in love with a cinema music orchestra that held its rehearsals in his neighborhood and, after persuading his parents to get him a set of bongos, started sitting in with the group. Soon he was invited to join, beginning a career in the film music business. To the consternation of his parents, rather than continuing on to college after graduating from high school he founded the Melody Cans, a group that played cover versions of current cinema hits. After becoming disenchanted with playing others' music, he disbanded the group and took a day job, but he soon re-formed the Melody Cans and enrolled in a diploma course in European classical music. This led to a position playing background music in Tamil̲ stage dramas. When Visu, the dramatist of the troupe, moved over to films he took Jude with him, rechristening him Vijaya Anand, literally, "victory ecstasy." Anand quickly became a sought-after music director and, while composing scores for films in several languages, is today best known for his work in the Kannaḍa cinema.

In 1992 a collection of Anand's film songs, *Dance Raja Dance,* was released. "When I Say Come/Ba Ennalu" (CD track 25) is a love duet performed by prominent playback singers S. P. Balasubrahmanyam and Manjula Guru. This release, on David Byrne's Luaka Bop label, brought Anand's music to an international audience that knew next to nothing about South Indian cinema but could delight in his urbane, polyglot, downright zany musical sensibility:

> Anand's compositions and arrangements gleefully gather the cliches of western pop and cheapen them into even gaudier tin emblems, melting them into a prickly conglomerate that doesn't give a hoot about homogeneity. The man's got a genius for flow, lustily careening at pinball velocity from intimations of jazz to imitations of mariachi, Eurodisco, heavy metal, flamenco, hiphop and bluegrass. . . . What sets Anand's productions apart from the *filmi* [cinema music] I'm used to is a juicy reliance on electronic technology that floats each song on a sea of synthesized sputters, coughs and gurgles, rendering even more improbable the romantic ballad fluttering beneath the foil. Such high-tech shenanigans liberate the genre a few vital inches from its foundation in colonial pop remnants by staking a self-conscious claim to India's rightful place in the collapsing modern world. (Tarte 1992, text in brackets added)

CROSS-CULTURAL COMPOSITION AND COLLABORATION

Outside the world of the cinema, over the last several decades Indian and non-Indian artists, sometimes working alone and sometimes together, have made numerous attempts to mix musical systems. The 1960s saw a worldwide burst of interest in the music of North India, largely because of the tremendous influence of one man, *sitārist* Ravi Shankar, who ironically termed rock's brief flirtation with India "the great *sitār* explosion" (Shankar 1968:92). Exceptional among popular musicians was former Beatles' guitarist George Harrison's (1943–2001) deep and abiding interest in the music of India and personal friendship and collaboration with Ravi Shankar, which stretched over three decades. Jazz musicians including John Coltrane, Bud Shank, Eric Dolphy, and John Handy became interested in the music of India during the 1960s, although few maintained an active interest over a long period of time (Farrell 1997:168–200). The profile of South Indian music in cross-cultural "fusion" has generally been lower than that of the music of North India. Best known is the collaboration of several South Indian musicians with English guitarist John McLaughlin and North Indian *tablā* drummer Zakir Hussain in two incarnations of the group Shakti beginning in the 1970s (for details of artists and recordings, see the Resources).

*"Can There Be Release/*Mōkṣamu Galadā*?" (CD Track 26).* Frank Bennett's haunting piano-vocal arrangement of Tyagaraja's *kriti*

FIGURE 5.5 *Photograph of Frank Bennett,* mridaṅgam, *and Geetha Ramanathan Bennett,* vīṇā. *(Courtesy of Frank Bennett)*

"Can There Be Release/*Mōkṣamu Galadā?*" on CD track 26 is a rare example of an attempt to marry a scheme of functional European harmony to a complete Karṇāṭak composition. Bennett, a composer and jazz drummer, studied Karṇāṭak vocal music and *vīṇā* with Dr. S. Ramanathan, *vīṇā* with M. A. Kalyanakrishnan Bhagavatar, and *mridaṅgam* with Ramnad V. Raghavan and T. Ranganathan. Since 1972 he has performed Karṇāṭak music with his wife, Geetha Ramanathan Bennett (Figure 5.5), the daughter of Dr. S. Ramanathan. Frank discussed the compositional challenges this project posed:

> One day Dr. Ramanathan said "I would like to teach you one of our most beautiful songs." It is one of Tyagaraja's great *kritis* about music. The text says, "Can anyone attain salvation without the knowledge of divine music?" Most Westerners will never encounter this piece; I thought by making an arrangement of it I'd be able to introduce it to Western audiences.
>
> Not all rāgas will work well with harmony. Some pentatonic rāgas don't give enough harmonic scope and some rāgas are so heavily laden with ornaments that putting them on a keyboard simply spoils

> the effect; the fixed notes of the piano wipe out the subtleties and shadings. You have to choose a rāga that can incorporate harmonies without destroying its subtle color. The rāga *Sāramati* has all seven tones in the ascent, then is pentatonic coming down. It lends itself to very tight clusters as well as open voicings, and it gave me both harmonic and contrapuntal possibilities to work with.
>
> Geetha sings this piece exactly as her father taught her, except for omitting some repeats. Writing the accompaniment, I tried to preserve the rāga's scalar structure in the outer voices at least, then looked for harmonic colors I thought would be appropriate for the meaning of the song. At some points, I wrote a bass line ascending stepwise while the treble line descends in pentatonic contrary motion. And I built three or four chordal combinations above each bass note—as many combinations as I could think of.
>
> In addition to providing color, the piano part had to take up the function of the *mridaṅgam*, to keep the time going. To achieve this I wrote some faster eighth note motion in the *anupallavi* and the second half of the *caraṇam*. In these places the *mridaṅgam* accompaniment typically becomes more intense, so I have the piano fill that role in these sections. Together with density, dynamics were also a consideration. Indian musicians do not usually discuss or teach dynamics, but they are a vital part of every shape, every song. My strategy was as the tessitura of the song broadens, as the melody goes up in register, the intensity should increase slightly (personal communication, August 16, 2001).

Before she sings the first line of text, vocalist Geetha Ramanathan Bennett's brief *ālāpana* outlines the *svaras* (beginning on *ri*) of the rāga in ascent, then in descent. In Activity 5.3, sing or play the scale of Sāramati rāga on an instrument, then as you begin listening to CD track 26 notice how her *ālāpana* follows—and creatively begins to depart from—the up and down pattern of this scalar sequence. A detailed listening guide to CD track 26 is available at http://www.wheatoncollege.edu/Faculty/MatthewAllen.html.

ACTIVITY 5.3 *Scale of Sāramati Rāga*

Ārōhaṇa *(ascent)*

sa	ri	ga	ma	pa	dha	ni	sā
C	D	E♭	F	G	A♭	B♭	C

Avarōhana *(descent)*

sā	ni	dha	ma	ga	sa
C	B♭	A♭	F	E♭	C

ACTIVITY 5.4. *Text and Translation, "Can There Be Release/*Mōkṣamu Galadā*?" (CD Track 26)*
Composed by Tyagaraja (1767–1847)
Rāga: Sāramati; Tāḷa: ādi (eight beat cycle); Geetha Ramanathan Bennett, vocalist; Mike Lang, piano

Pallavi (close translation)	(Freer translation)
Mōkṣamu galadā bhuvilō jīvan Can there be release in this world *Muktulu kāni vāralaku* For those who are not liberated in this body?	Can there be release in this world for those who are not liberated in this body?
Anupallavi *Sākṣātkāra nī sad bhakti* O god present before me! for those who are lacking in real devotion to you,	O god present before me! For those who are lacking in real devotion to you
Saṃgīta jñāna vihīnulaku (mōkṣamu . . .) And who lack knowledge of the mystery of music (can there be release . . .)	And who lack knowledge of the mystery of music (Can there be release . . .)
Caraṇam *Prāṇānala saṃyōgamu valla* Through the commingling of breath and fire	O god praised by Tyagaraja!
Praṇava nādamu sapta svaramulai paraga The sound of *om* itself becomes the seven musical notes,	Such people don't know the nature of your mind When you're immersed in playing the *vīṇā*

Vīṇā vādana lōluḍau śiva mano
When you are immersed in
playing the *vīṇā*, Śiva.
Vidham erugaru tyāgarāja vinuta
(mōkṣamu . . .)
Those (who don't know the
mysteries of music)
don't know the nature of
your mind, O god praised
by Tyagaraja (can there be
release . . .)

And the sound of *om* itself
becomes the seven notes
Through the commingling of
breath and fire
(Can there be release . . .)

[Translated from the Telugu by Phillip B. Wagoner]

TATVA, A REGIONAL PERFORMANCE TRADITION IN KARṆĀṬAKA STATE

The Deccan Plateau: Meeting of North and South India. The states of Karṇāṭaka and Āndhra Pradesh form a geographical and cultural bridge between South and North India. Their northern sections extend into the Deccan Plateau, historically a meeting ground for religions, languages, and artistic forms from North and South. In northern Karṇāṭaka, where CD track 27, a philosophical genre of song called *tatva*, was recorded, many people speak the North Indian languages Marāṭhī and Hindi in addition to the official state language Kannaḍa. Members of the large Muslim community in Karṇāṭaka and Āndhra Pradesh also speak Urdu, structurally very close to Hindi but written in Arabic script and containing a large number of Persian language loan words.

Karṇāṭaka has been central to the history of Karṇāṭak music and has spawned many great Hindustāni musicians as well. The Vijayanagar kingdom was the home of the "father" of Karṇāṭak music Purandara Dasa and was the major site of patronage for South Indian music before its disintegration in the mid-sixteenth century. The Mahārājas of Mysore were great patrons of music up until the absorption of Mysore state into newly independent India in 1948. They supported Karṇāṭak as well as European music and maintained a European orchestra at court alongside a retinue of Karṇāṭak musicians. The last Māhāraja of Mysore was a great lover of European classical music and, among other philanthropic activities, personally underwrote the recordings of a range of works by the Russian composers Lyapanov, Medtner, and Scriabin. Nearby Bangalore, the "Silicon Valley" of South India, is today a major center of Karṇāṭak music.

The state of Āndhra Pradesh has a similarly hybrid cultural history. Major Muslim kingdoms existed for centuries in the northern part of the state, the largest being Hyderabad, which maintained an independent identity up until Indian independence. Āndhra Pradesh was home to the great Hindu composer of *saṅkīrtana* Tallapaka Annamacarya, and the ancestors of Tyagaraja were among the many families of artists and scholars who migrated from Āndhra Pradesh south to Tañjāvūr after the disintegration of the Vijayanagar Empire and the assumption of rule in Tañjāvūr by a lineage of Telugu kings in 1565. Today a wide spectrum of musical traditions is practiced in the state (Roghair, in Arnold 2000:889–902).

The Kannaḍa Tatva *Composer Sharif Saheb.* Regional folk music traditions are found in all the South Indian states and are crucial in local communities' expression of their identity and history. Important performance genres in Karṇāṭaka are congregational *bhajan* singing similar to CD track 1; the Kannaḍa language dance-drama *Yakṣagāna*; women's life cycle songs; political, moral, and ethical songs sung by male specialists; songs predicting the future; and the philosophical solo song genre *tatva*. *Tatvas* range from expressions of sectarian Hinduism to more general and universal spiritual messages. Sharif Saheb, the early twentieth-century composer of the *tatva* "Why Do You Worry/*Yāke cinti?*" (CD track 27), was from the village of Sisunala, fifteen miles from Dharwar town in northern Karṇāṭaka. A young boy from a Muslim family, he was taken under the wing of Govinda Bhatta, a Brahmin who became his *guru* and endured censure by his own community for performing the sacred thread ceremony for his young Muslim protege. He composed nonsectarian songs on universal themes that remain popular with Kannaḍa-speaking people of all religious backgrounds.

Hindu–Muslim Relations in Karṇāṭaka State. Anthropologist M. N. Srinivas conducted extended fieldwork in a small multicaste village in southern Karṇāṭaka between 1948 and 1952. Muslims were the third largest group in the village at this time, providing occupational specialties that knit them closely into the majority Hindu community.

At the time of Srinivas' fieldwork relations between Muslims and Hindus were extremely tense throughout South Asia—the 1947 riots accompanying the partition of India and Pakistan had taken hundreds of thousands of lives—but in the village Srinivas found amicable relations and long-standing friendships across religious communal lines:

> Relations between Hindus and Muslims were close. I was occasionally surprised at the intimate knowledge which some Muslims had of Hindu culture. Karim, for instance, was well informed about the divisions among Peasants [prosperous non-Brahmin Hindu landowner-cultivators], their wedding customs, etc. I have already mentioned Akbar Sab's interest in putting an end to my single-blessedness [bachelorhood] and the criteria he looked for in the bride would have won the approval of my Peasant friends. I found a few Muslims enjoying listening to gramophone records of dramas which were based on stories taken from the corpus of Hindu mythology. And one of the finest actors on the Kannaḍa stage in the twenties and thirties was Peer who played leading roles in dramas based on stories from Hindu mythology. He was universally admired by the Hindus for the sensitivity with which he played those roles.
>
> On the other side, some Hindus admired certain traits of Muslim culture. For example, Rame Gowda praised the brevity, dignity, and quietness of a Muslim wedding which was a striking contrast to the elaborate, noisy and chaotic Hindu counterpart. He thought that Muslims displayed and served their food aesthetically, while Hindus paid no attention to these aspects. . . .
>
> Friendship cut across not only castes but religious divisions as well. The Potter Sannayya and Karim were such good friends that even their wives had become close companions. Their houses were close to each other, separated only by the width of Gudi street. I once asked the Potter how it was that he and Karim were great friends, and he replied that his father and Karim's father had both been good friends in the old days. . . . Shukoor who owned the hire-cycle shop was a friend of Swamy, Nadu Gowda's son. Once Shukoor returned from a brief trip to a nearby town and immediately after, he went in search of Swamy. Shukoor explained to me that if he did not see his friend for a few days he became uneasy in his mind. Such declarations of affection were frequently heard between grown men. (Srinivas 1976:206–207; text in brackets added)

Kathā Performers of the Kinnaṛi Jōgi *Community.* An important category of regional musician in Karṇāṭaka is the *alamāri,* mendicant alms-seeker. That their musical knowledge is transmitted orally does not imply that *alamāri* learn casually; many performers are formally initiated and apprenticed, similar to classical performers. Nor is their alms-seeking viewed as begging in the pejorative sense, but rather as an act of worldly renunciation, devotion, and community service—much like the practice of *uñcavritti bhajana* by Tyagaraja and his disciples discussed in Chapter 1.

The majority of Karṇāṭaka's regional musicians are *dālits* (formerly known as "untouchables"). The musicians heard in CD track 27 are *jōgis*, a name also found in the North Indian states of Rajasthan and Madhya Pradesh. *Jōgis* are similar to the Bauls of Bengal in the manner in which they recruit members from lower Hindu castes and Muslim communities. The *jōgi* musicians of Karṇāṭaka are Hindus who are knowledgeable of Muslim traditions and language. The performers take the name *kinnaṛi jōgis* from the two-stringed chordophone they play (Figure 5.6). The strings are stretched along a horizontal stick to which three resonator gourds are also attached; an additional vertical stick serves as a portable instrument stand. *Kinnaṛi jōgis* are the only ones to perform *kathā* lengthy story narratives. *Kathās* include genres such as the

FIGURE 5.6 Jōgis *alms-seeking while playing* kinnaṛi. *(Courtesy of Gayathri Rajapur Kassebaum)*

bhakti compositions of Purandara Dasa and philosophical *tatva* songs. Throughout a *kathā* performance *jōgis* inject regular doses of humor and address the everyday concerns of their mostly rural audiences.

*"Why Do You Worry/*Yāke Cinti?*" (CD Track 27).* Guddappa Jogi is a prominent and articulate member of the north Karṇāṭaka *jōgi* community. He makes his living from entertaining farmers and small businessmen, mostly in the rural districts where he travels regularly. In "Why Do You Worry/*Yāke Cinti?*" Guddappa Jogi and his fellow singer and brother-in-law N. Guddappa alternate initiating lines of the song. His cousins Gudeppa and Sivalingappa provide harmonium drone, small cymbals called *tāḷam,* and responsorial singing to help create a performer-audience dialogue in performance (Figure 5.7).

The rhythmic framework of "Why Do You Worry" is duple (the musicians do not think of it as being in a particular tāḷa). The formal structure of the song is somewhat similar to *saṅkīrtanam* (Chapter 1) in that the musicians periodically return to a *pallavi*-like refrain (labeled A in Activity 5.6) between successive stanzas. Gayathri Rajapur Kassebaum

FIGURE 5.7 *Photograph of Guddappa Jogi (center) with N. Guddappa, Gudeppa, and Sivalingappa, performing in formal setting.* (Courtesy Gayathri Rajapur Kassebaum)

finds the use of melodies derived from North Indian rāgas quite common in the singing of *jōgis,* testifying to the pervasiveness of Hindustāni music traditions in northern Karṇāṭaka (personal communication, 2001). While the musicians do not think of "Why Do You Worry?" as being in a rāga, its melody bears a strong resemblance to Hindustāni Bhairavi rāga, whose scalar summary (Activity 5.5)—but not its ornamentation or phrase structure—is identical to Tōḍi rāga in Karṇāṭak music (Activity 4.3). The musicians alternate between two distinct melodic lines throughout the performance. A detailed listening guide to CD track 27 is available at http://www.wheatoncollege.edu/Faculty/Matthew-Allen.html.

ACTIVITY 5.5 *Scalar Summary of Hindustāni Bhairavi Rāga*

Ārōhaṇa *(ascent)*

sa	ri	ga	ma	pa	dha	ni	s̄a
C	D♭	E♭	F	G	A♭	B♭	C

Avarōhaṇa *(descent)*

s̄a	ni	dha	pa	ma	ga	ri	sa
C	B♭	A♭	G	F	E♭′	D♭′	C

ACTIVITY 5.6 *Text and Translation, "Why Do You Worry/ Yāke Cinti?" (CD Track 27)*
Composed by Sharif Saheb (early twentieth century); translated from the Kannaḍa by Gayathri Rajapur Kassebaum. Guddappa Jogi and N. Guddappa, vocalists; Gudeppa and Sivalingappa, harmonium, tāḷam cymbals, and responsorial singing.

Note: The performers sing the lines of text in the following order: A A B B C A D E A F F E G H A

A.	*(Refrain) Yāke cinti māduti yele manavē ninna, yātara sukha idu yelu manavē*	Why do you worry, hey you mind? what kind of happiness is this, hey you mind?

B.	*Yārigu yārilla yelu manavē ninna, mūru dinada santi yelu manavē*	Who is there for you? no one, hey you mind (i.e., no one can help you when your mind is tormented); life is short, like a three-day transaction in a busy market place
C.	*Bāllantha hiriyaru hēluva mātidu, allan tyanu byādalu manavē ninna, yātara sukha idu yelu manavē*	These are the words of the experienced soul; don't doubt it, hey you mind, hey you; what kind of happiness is this, hey you mind?
D.	*Lōkanāthana pāda bekādare, sahakāra mādiko yelu manavē ninna, yātara sukhavidu yelu manavē*	If you need the grace of the supreme (literally, if you need the feet of Śiva lōkanātha, lord of the world), ease toward him, hey you mind; what kind of happiness is this, hey you mind?
E.	*Sēradavara munde jāri biddante, harateya kochabyada yele manavē ninna, yātara sukhavidu yelu manavē*	It is like slipping and falling in front of the opponents; don't engage in idle talk, hey you mind; what kind of happiness is this, hey you mind?
F.	*Kallantyanu byādalu manavē ninna, sulantyanu byādalu manavē*	Don't steal, hey you mind, hey you; don't lie, hey you mind?
G.	*Hēsige samsara yelu manavē ninna, yestu hēsu janma tirugi bandi yelu manavē*	Worldly existence *(samsara)* is sometimes ugly, hey you mind; how many ugly life cycles have you gone through, hey you mind?

H. *Dēshakke dituvadā vāsulli sisunāla, guru gōvindana pāda ondu manavē ninna, yātara sukhavidu yelu manavē*	Be truthful in this world, as Sisunala (*mudrā* of Sharif Saheb, the composer) says; embrace the feet of the Guru Govinda, hey you mind, hey you mind; what kind of happiness is this, hey you mind?

A Circle Completed. The renunciation of worldly possessions, as well as religiously sanctioned alms-seeking—such as Tyagaraja's *uñcavritti bhajana*—have for centuries been regarded as exemplary models for behavior in India. Purandara Dasa in the fifteenth century and Tyagaraja in the eighteenth followed this path, one that *kinnaṛi jōgis* are attempting to walk with dignity into the twenty-first century. Guddappa Jogi finds the current climate difficult for *jōgis* to continue their traditional profession. In the face of criticism and misunderstanding, he and his colleagues have formed a group and have worked to diversify their activity to include not just alms-seeking in villages but performance in more formal situations as well.

> At present, many unauthorized persons seek alms. Some are liars and phony people who make begging their profession. The authorized and religiously sanctioned alms seekers had a greater mission in life. They were the missionaries who imparted the moral, historical ethical values to the communities. They condemned the ills of human nature and praised the merits through their musical performances. But these new beggars cannot be compared with us. We are the traditional alms seekers of our community. . . . We don't mind if as little as one *rupee* is given as alms, but we want the people to respect our art and us as alms seekers. We are religiously sanctioned alms seekers, and this profession has been passed down to us from our fathers. Because of these reasons, we have formed a performing group to earn our living not based solely on alms seeking, but by performing our art as a group. (Guddappa Jogi, translated in Kassebaum 1994:299–300)

Guddappa Jogi validates his community's alms-seeking in one story narrative by linking their lineage to Arjuna, one of the five Pāṇḍava brothers in the epic *Mahābhārata*. In penance for a sin unwittingly committed, Arjuna was sent to wander the earth for twelve years. Just before the period of exile was to finish, Arjuna could no longer stand the separation from his family. He was advised by seven *gurus* to visit his mother disguised as a *jōgi*, and in the train of events that followed was also happily reunited with his wife. As he was about to take the *kinnaṛi* that had served him well and let it float away down a river,

> At that time, there was a poor man standing at the river bend. Seeing Arjuna discarding the instrument and his alms bag he asked him to give them to him so that he could wear the clothes that Arjuna had worn, and carry the *kinnaṛi* and alms bag. This poor man had a family of his own. He made all of his brothers *jōgis*. That is how our community originated. (Guddappa Jogi, translated in Kassebaum 1994:290)

SUMMARY

Our intent in this chapter has been to open doors to South Indian music beyond the Karṇāṭak concert world, including regional folk traditions, dance and drama, cinema music, and cross-cultural collaboration. The topics we could cover can only be suggestive of the immense variety of artistic forms practiced today by South Indians. We hope that the reader has found within this book the seeds to engagement with the music and the people of South India; the materials listed in the Resources are designed to facilitate further exploration.

Glossary

Abhināya Mimetic gesture language

Akṣarā Individual beat or count (a component of tāḷa)

Alamāri Mendicant alms-seeker; category of musical performers of Karṇāṭaka

***Ālāpana* (sometimes called *rāgam*)** Melodic improvisation in free rhythm

Ambā "Mother"; term for goddess, associated with Pārvatī in particular

Aṅga "Limb"; a group of *akṣarās*, component of tāḷa

Anupallavi "Continuation of the sprouting"; second section of kriti and other genres

Ārādhana Festival, celebration

Araṅgēṟṟam Debut performance

Ārōhaṇa Ascending direction of a rāga

Avarōhaṇa Descending direction of a rāga

Bhajan Devotional song

Bhakti Devotional love

Bharata nāṭyam Concert dance form that evolved from former temple and court dance

Bhava Feeling (as in *rāga bhava*)

Brahmā One of the three major Hindu gods; spouse of Sarasvatī

Brahmin The first of the four *varṇas* in Indian social theory

Brikka Fast speed vocal or instrumental musical passages

Caraṇam "Foot"; stanza; third section of *kriti* and other genres

Caste Social grouping based on birth; from Portuguese *casta,* "lineage or breed" (see *jāti, varṇa*)

Dālit, Ādi drāviḍa "Scheduled castes"; terms for social groups outside of and functionally below the conceptual four-*varṇa* system of Indian society (formerly called "untouchables")

Dēvadāsi Literally, servant, *dāsi*, of god, *dēva*; a community of women renowned for music and dance skills, attached in hereditary service to Hindu temples and royal courts

Dēvī Generic term for goddess

Gamaka Grace, gracefulness; closest English cognate is "ornament" or "ornamentation"

Gaṇēśa (also called Gaṇanātha) Elephant-headed god, one of the two sons of Śiva

Ghaṭam An open-top tuned clay pot idiophone

Gītam Simple composition, foundational part of Karṇāṭak students' training

Guru Teacher, preceptor

Hanumān A god, faithful companion of Rāma and renowned as a master singer

Jaṇṭa Stress; one of the three major classes of *gamaka*

Jāru Slide; one of the three major classes of *gamaka*

Jāti "Variety"; (a) social grouping based on birth, a subdivision of *varṇa*; (b) the five important numerical varieties of Karṇāṭak rhythm (4,3,7,5,9)

Jāvaḷi Dance music genre; love song, often addressed to a human patron

Jōgi A community of *alamāri* mendicant musicians in Karṇāṭaka

Kaccēri "Court"; music concert

Kampita Shake or oscillation; one of the three major classes of *gamaka*

Kaṇakku Arithmetic or calculation; important mode of rhythmic thinking (see also *sarva laghu*)

Kañjīra Small lizardskin frame drum with metal jingles attached to a wooden shell

Kathā Lengthy story narratives of Karṇāṭak

Kathakaḷi "Story-play"; dance-drama form of Kēraḷa

Kīrtana, kīrtanam Broadly, a synonym for *kriti*; often used in reference to relatively simple *kritis* performed with a greater emphasis on devotion than virtuosity

Kriti Three-part compositional form, central genre of Karṇāṭak concert tradition (see also *kīrtana*)

Kṛṣṇa A god; one of the ten incarnations of Viṣṇu

Kṣatriya The second of the four varṇas in Indian social theory

Lakṣmī (also called Śrī) A goddess; spouse of Viṣṇu, associated with prosperity, well-being, royal power, illustriousness

Madhyama kāla Middle speed; twice the rhythmic density of *vilamba kāla*

Mahābhārata Sanskrit epic; considered *smriti*, remembered and written down

Mangaḷa iśai Auspicious music

Manōdharma saṅgīta Improvised music

Mantra Sacred syllable or syllables

Mēḷakartā Symmetrical classificatory scheme of seventy-two musical scales

Morsing Jaw harp idiophone

Mridaṅgam Double-headed jackwood membranophone, the main drum in Karṇāṭak music

Mudrā (a) Mimetic gesture; (b) composer's signature, typically inserted toward the end of the caraṇam section of a *kriti*

Murugan Ancient Tamiḻ god, incorporated into Sanskritic Hinduism as one of the two sons of Śiva

Nāgasvaram Long double-reed aerophone used in *periya mēḷam*

Naṭarāja A god; a form of Śiva historically associated with Cidambaram

Nāṭya Umbrella term for drama-dance-music (Sanskrit)

Niraval Improvisation of a new melodic setting for a line of a *kriti* while keeping its rhythmic structure substantially intact

Ōduvār Vocalists who perform *tēvāram* hymns in Śiva temples

Padam (a) Dance music genre in *bharata nāṭyam*, love song addressed to a deity, usually considered an allegory for religious devotion; (b) in *Kathakaḷi*, song genre that carries the first-person dialogue of the play and occupies the majority of a play's duration

Pallavi "Sprouting"; first section of *kriti, padam, jāvaḷi*, and other genres

Pārvatī A goddess; spouse and *śakti* of Śiva

Periya mēḷam "Great" or "important" temple music ensemble, built around *nāgasvaram* and *tavil*

Pūja Religious rituals, prayers

Purandara Dāsa Sixteenth-century composer and pedagogue revered as the Father of Karṇāṭak music

Rādhā A goddess; consort of Kṛṣṇa

Rāga Melodic mode

Rāgam-tānam-pallavi Set of improvisational genres built on a brief composed theme

Rāma A god; one of the ten incarnations of Viṣṇu

Rāmāyaṇa Sanskrit epic; considered *smriti*, remembered and written down

Rasa "Juice"; sentiment, aesthetic potential; related to *rasika*, dedicated connoisseur

Sabhā Arts-presenting organization

Śaivite Devotee of Śiva

Sakhī Female confidante of the heroine in dance music genres

Śakti "Embodied power"; term for goddess, special association with Pārvatī as consort of Śiva

Samam First beat of a tāḷa cycle

Saṅkīrtanam Compositional genre that historically preceded *kriti*

Sanskrit Ancient Indo-Aryan language in which the *Vēdas*, epics *Rāmāyaṇa* and *Mahābhārata*, and much dramatic literature and poetry are composed

Saraḷi variśai Basic set of melodic-rhythmic exercises in Karṇāṭak music, developed by Purandara Dāsa

Sarasvatī A goddess; patroness of the arts and learning, spouse of Brahmā

Sarva laghu Time flow; important mode of rhythmic thinking (see also *kaṇakku*)

Sītā A goddess, spouse of Rāma, revered as ideal wife

Śiva One of the three major Hindu gods; spouse of Pārvati

Solkaṭṭu "Bundles of syllables"; used for rhythmic recitation and conceptualization

Śriṅgāra rasa Erotic sentiment, enacted through *abhināya* in dance music genres

Śruti (a) Sense of pitch, intonation; (b) tonal center, tonic; (c) steady melodic drone background; (d) something heard directly (c.f. *Vēdas*); (e) *śruti peṭṭi, śruti* "box," bellows-operated instrument, provides background drone

Śudra The fourth of the four *varṇas* in Indian social theory

Svara "Radiating self"; constituent melodic unit of rāga containing elements of pitch and *gamaka*; closest English cognate is the word "note"

Svara kalpana "Invented" or "created" *svaras*, improvisation based on solfège syllables

Tāḷa Rhythmic cycle

Tāḷam Small hand-held cymbals used in many performance genres

Tambūra Long-necked lute chordophone, provides background *śruti* drone in concerts

Tamiḻ Iśai "Tamiḻ Music"; (a) body of Tamiḻ language musical compositions; (b) twentieth-century movement promoting and disseminating this music

Tāṇḍava Vigorous style of dancing (as in the dance of Śiva), usually gendered as masculine

Tani āvarttanam Drum solo

Tatva Philosophical genre of song in Karṇāṭaka

Tavil Double-headed membranophone used in *periya mēḷam*

Tēvāram Sixth- to eighth-century A.D. Tamiḻ hymns, performed by *ōduvār* vocalists in Śiva temples

Trīmūrti "Trinity"; renowned group of Karṇāṭak composers: Syama Sastri, Tyagaraja, and Muttusvami Dikshitar

Tyāṇi Sacred song in Kēraḷa temple vocal repertoire

Uñcavritti bhajana Devotional songs sung while going from house to house

Upaniṣads Expositions on the essence of the Vēdas

Vaiṣṇavite Devotee of Viṣṇu

Vaiśya The third of the four *varṇas* in Indian social theory

Vakra "Crooked"; movement in a rāga that deviates from stepwise scalar fashion

Varṇa "Color"; in Indian social theory, four overarching hereditarily determined categories

Vēdas Oldest texts of Hinduism, considered *śruti*, heard directly from the gods by early sages

Vilamba kāla Slow speed, half the rhythmic density of *madhyama kāla*

Vīṇā Primary indigenous South Indian chordophone, fretted, with four main playing strings

Viṣṇu One of the three major Hindu gods, spouse of Lakṣmi

Yōga Form of physical and spiritual discipline; more broadly, a wide range of activities that link (yoke) one to the divine

Resources

Reading

Allen, Matthew Harp. *The Tamil Padam: A Dance Music Genre of South India* (Ph.D. dissertation, Wesleyan University). Ann Arbor, MI: University Microfilms, 1992.

———. "Rewriting the Script for South Indian Dance." *TDR: The Drama Review (Journal of Performance Studies)* 41(3):63–100, 1997.

———. "Tales Tunes Tell: Deepening the Dialogue Between "Classical" and "Non-Classical" in the Music of South India." *Yearbook for Traditional Music* 30:22–52, 1998.

Arnold, Alison, "Film Music: Northern Area." In *The Garland Encyclopedia of World Music, Volume Five, South Asia*, ed. Alison Arnold. New York/London: Garland Publishing, 2000:531–541.

Baskaran, S. Theodore. *The Eye of the Serpent: An Introduction to Tamil Cinema*. Madras: East West Books Pvt Ltd., 1996.

Benjamin, Walter. "The Work of Art in the Age of Mechanical Reproduction" (1935). In *Selected Writings, vol. 3 (1935–1938)*, ed. Howard Eiland and Michael W. Jennings. Cambridge: Belknap Press, 2002.

Catlin, Amy. "Pallavi and Kriti of Karnatak Music: Evolutionary Processes and Survival Strategies." *National Centre for the Performing Arts (NCPA), Bombay, Quarterly Journal* XIV(1):26–44, 1985.

Claus, Peter, Sarah Diamond, and Margaret Mills, editors. *South Asian Folklore: An Encyclopedia*. New York/London: Routledge, 2002.

Coomaraswamy, Ananda. *The Dance of Śiva: Essays on Indian Art and Culture*. New York: Dover Publications, 1985 (originally published 1918).

Cutler, Norman. *Songs of Experience: The Poetics of Tamil Devotion*. Bloomington and Indianapolis: Indiana University Press, 1987.

Dirks, Nicholas B. *Castes of Mind: Colonialism and the Making of Modern India*. Princeton, NJ: Princeton University Press, 2001.

Eck, Diana. *Darśan: Seeing the Divine Image in India*. New York: Columbia University Press, 1998.

Farrell, Gerry. *Indian Music and the West*. Oxford: Clarendon Press, 1997.

Gough, Catherine. *Caste in a Tanjore Village. Aspects of Caste in South India, Ceylon and North-West Pakistan*, ed. E. R. Leach. Cambridge: Cambridge University Press, 1971:11–60.

Greene, Paul D. "Film Music: Southern Area." In *The Garland Encyclopedia of World Music, Volume Five, South Asia*, ed. Alison Arnold. New York/London: Garland Publishing, 2000:542–546.

Groesbeck, Rolf, and Joseph J. Palackal. "Kerala." In *The Garland Encyclopedia of World Music, Volume Five, South Asia*, ed. Alison Arnold. New York/London: Garland Publishing, 2000:929–951.

Irschick, Eugene. *Tamil Revivalism in the 1930s*. Chennai: Cre-A, 1986.

Jackson, William J. *Tyagaraja: Life and Lyrics*. Madras: Oxford University Press, 1991.

———. *Tyagaraja and the Renewal of Tradition: Translations and Reflections*. Delhi: Motilal Banarsidass, 1994.

Jairazbhoy, Nazir. *Hi-Tech Shiva, and Other Apocryphal Stories*. Van Nuys: Apsara Media, 1991. An "academic allegory" on scholars as "the new Gods pursuing their selfish ends under the rubric of scholarship."

Jones, Clifford R., and Betty True Jones. *Kathakali: An introduction to the Dance-Drama of Kerala*. Designed and with photographs by Jan Steward. San Francisco: American Society for Eastern Arts, 1970.

Kassebaum, Gayathri Rajapur. *Katha: Six Performance Traditions and the Preservation of Group Identity in Karnataka, South India* (Ph.D. dissertation, University of Washington). Ann Arbor, MI: University Microfilms, 1994.

Kersenboom, Saskia. *Nityasumangali: Devadasi Tradition in South India*. Delhi: Motilal Banarsidass, 1987.

Meduri, Avanthi. *Bharatha Natyam: What Are You?* In *Moving History/Dancing Cultures: A Dance History Reader*, ed. Ann Dils and Ann Cooper Albright. Middletown, CT: Wesleyan University Press, 2001.

Narayan, R. K. "Selvi." In *Malgudi Days*. New York: Viking Press, 1982:155–165. Short story about a Karṇāṭak singer and her husband/manager.

Nelson, David. *Mrdangam Mind: The Tani Avartanam in Karnatak Music* (Ph.D. dissertation, Wesleyan University). Ann Arbor, MI: University Microfilms, 1991 (see affililated listing under Viewing).

Nelson, David. "Karnatak Tala." In *The Garland Encyclopedia of World Music, Volume Five, South Asia*, ed. Alison Arnold. New York/London: Garland Publishing, 2000:138–161.

Neuman, Daniel. *The Life of Music in North India: The Organization of an Artistic Tradition*. Chicago: University of Chicago Press, 1990 (originally published 1980).

Palackal, Joseph J. "India: Christian Music." In *The New Grove Dictionary of Music and Musicians, vol. 12*. London: Macmillan Publishers, 2001:233–234.

Pesch, Ludwig. *The Illustrated Companion to South Indian Classical Music.* Delhi: Oxford University Press, 1999.
Peterson, Indira Viswanathan. *Poems to Śiva: The Hymns of the Tamil Saints.* Princeton, NJ: Princeton University Press, 1989.
Raghavan, V. *The Power of the Sacred Name: V. Raghavan's Studies in Namasiddhanta and Indian Culture* (Studies in Indian Tradition, No. 4), ed. William J. Jackson. Columbia, MO: South Asia Books, 1994.
Ramanuja Ayyangar, Ariyakkudi. "The Concert Tradition." In *Ariyakkudi Ramanuja Ayyangar Centenary Souvenir*. Chennai: n.p., 1990.
Ramanujan, A. K. *Poems of Love and War, from the Eight Anthologies and the Ten Long Poems of Classical Tamil.* New York: Columbia University Press, 1985.
Ramanujan, A. K., Velcheru Narayana Rao, and David Shulman. *When God Is a Customer: Telugu Courtesan Songs by Ksetrayya and Others.* Berkeley: University of California Press, 1994.
Reck, David. "Music Instruments: Southern Area." In *The Garland Encyclopedia of World Music, Volume V, South Asia*, New York/London: Garland Publishing, 2000:350–369.
Roghair, Gene. "Andhra Pradesh." In *The Garland Encyclopedia of World Music, Volume V, South Asia*, ed. Alison Arnold. New York/London: Garland Publishing, 2000:889–902.
Roy, Arundhati. *The God of Small Things*. New York: Random House, 1997. Contains detailed description of a Kathakaḷi performance.
Sambamurthy, P. *South Indian Music Book*, Vol. II, 7th ed. Madras: Indian Music Publishing House, 1968.
Sankaran, T., and Matthew Allen. "The Social Organization of Music and Musicians: Southern Area." In *The Garland Encyclopedia of World Music, Volume Five, South Asia*, ed. Alison Arnold. New York/London: Garland Publishing, 2000:383–396.
Shankar, Ravi. *My Music, My Life*. New York: Simon & Schuster, 1968.
Sherinian, Zoe. "Dalit Theology in Tamil Christian Folk Music: A Transformative Liturgy by James Theophilus Appavoo." In *Popular Christianity in India: Riting Between the Lines*, ed. Selva Raj and and Corinne Dempsey. Albany: SUNY Press, 2002.
Singer, Milton. *When a Great Tradition Modernizes: An Anthropological Approach to Indian Civilization*. New York: Praeger, 1972.
Srinivas, M. N. *The Remembered Village*. Berkeley: University of California Press, 1976.
Subramaniam, V. *The Sacred and the Secular in India's Performing Arts: Ananda K. Coomaraswamy Centenary Essays*. Columbia, MO: South Asia Books, 1983.
Sundaram, B. M. *Palaiyazhi: Musical Scales*. Chennai: Murali Ravali Art Centre, 1979.

Sundaram, B. M. *Harikatha: Its Origin and Development*. Bangalore: R. K. Srikantan Trust, 2001.

Sundaram, B. M. *Marabu Thantha Manikkangal (Traditional Bharata Natyam Dancers of Tamil Nadu)*. Chennai: Dr. V. Raghavan Centre for Performing Arts, 2003. (In Tamil; English edition in preparation.)

Tarte, Bob. "Songs for Uninvited Guests." *The Beat* (magazine) 11:3, 1992.

Terada, Yoshitaka. *Multiple Interpretations of a Charismatic Individual: The Case of the Great Nagasvaram Musician, T. N. Rajarattinam Pillai*. (Ph.D. dissertation, University of Washington). Ann Arbor, MI: University Microfilms, 1992.

———. "T. N. Rajarattinam Pillai and Caste Rivalry in South Indian Classical Music." *Ethnomusicology* 44(3):460–490, 2000.

Tharu, Susie, and K. Lalita. *Women Writing in India: 600 B.C. to the Present. Volume I: 600 B.C. to the Early 20th Century*. New York: The Feminist Press, 1991.

Viswanathan, T. "Presidential Address by Vidwan T. Viswanathan." *Journal of the Music Academy, Madras* LX:9–17, 1989.

Viswanathan, T., and Jody Cormack. "Melodic Improvisation in Karnatak Music: The Manifestations of Raga." In *In the Course of Performance: Studies in the World of Musical Improvisation*, ed. Bruno Nettl and Melinda Russell. Chicago: University of Chicago Press, 1998.

Weidman, Amanda Jane. *Questions of Voice: On the Subject of "Classical" Music in South India* (Ph.D. dissertation, anthropology, Columbia University). Ann Arbor, MI: University Microfilms, 2001.

Widdess, Richard. *The Ragas of Early Indian Music: Modes, Melodies and Musical Notations from the Gupta Period to c. 1250*. Oxford: Clarendon Press, 1995.

Wolf, Richard K. "Three Perspectives on Music and the Idea of Tribe in India," and "Mourning Songs and Human Pasts Among the Kotas of South India." *Tribal Music in India*, special issue of *Asian Music* 32(1), Fall/Winter 2001.

Wolf, Richard K., and Zoe Sherinian. "Tamil Nadu." In *In The Garland Encyclopedia of World Music, Volume V, South Asia*, ed. Alison Arnold. New York/London: Garland Publishing, 2000:903–928.

Zarrilli, Phillip. *Kathakali*. In *Indian Theatre: Traditions of Performance*, ed. Farley Richmond, Darius Swann, and Phillip Zarrilli. Honolulu: University of Hawaii Press, 1990.

———. *Kathakali Dance-Drama: Where Gods and Demons Come to Play*. London/New York: Routledge, 2000 (also see affiliated listings under Viewing).

Listening

Karṇāṭak and Devotional

Kanyakumari, A., violin. *Vadya Lahari (Waves of Music)*. Music of the World. www.rootsworld.com/rw/motw.

Karnataka College of Percussion. *River Yamuna.* Music of the World.
Krishnan, Ramnad, vocalist. *Vidwan. Music of South India. Songs of the Carnatic Tradition.* Nonesuch Explorer Recordings.
Muktha, T., vocalist. *Vintage Reminiscences: Padams & Javalis.* Carnatica Archival Centre. www.carnatica.com/arcade-main.htm.
Palackal, Joseph, producer. *Qambel Māran: Syriac Chants from South India.* PAN Records. www.indussociety.org/cmsindia.
Ramani, N., flute. *Lotus Signatures.* Music of the World.
———. *Ragas Kannada, Kalyanavasanta, Natakuranji, Ranjani, Des.* Nimbus Records. www.nimbusrecords.com.
Ravikiran, Chitravina N., *chitravīṇā* (lute). *Music from Madras.* Nimbus Records.
Sankaran, Trichy, *mridaṅgam* and *kanjīra. Laya Vinyas: Indian Drumming.* Music of the World.
Staal, Frits, and John Levy, producers. *The Four Vedas.* Smithsonian Folkways Recordings. www.folkways.si.edu.
Subramaniam, Karaikudi, *vīṇā. Sunada.* Music of the World.
Venkateswarlu, Voleti, vocalist. *Voleti and Friends: Vijayawada 1963.* Apsara Media for Intercultural Education, 13659 Victory Boulevard, Suite #577, Van Nuys, CA 91401, fax: 818-785-1495.
Viswanathan, T., flute. *Tribute.* Performing and Media Arts. soltes@mindspring.com.
Viswanathan, T., flute. *South Indian Classical Flute: Tanjor Viswanathan.* JVC World Sounds Special VICG 5453.

Cinema and Cross-Cultural Composition/Performance

Anand, Vijaya. *Dance Raja Dance. Asia Classics I: The South Indian Film Music of Vijaya Anand.* www.luakabop.com/asia_classics/cmp/index1.html.
Ilaiyaraja, A. R. Rahman (film music composers; many recordings available through Internet purchase links listed in Other).
Lewis, Lezz, and Hariharan. *Colonial Cousins.* Magnasound. www.colonial-cousins.com.
Mani, Madurai G. S. *Karnatak Isaiyum Cinemavum (Karṇāṭak Music and the Cinema).* Inreco Audio Cassettes PRT C-1004,1005. www.saigan.com/inreco.
McLaughlin, John, guitar; L. Shankar, violin; Zakir Hussain, *tablā*; T.H. Vinayakram, *ghaṭam. The Best of Shakti.* Moment Records.
Raghavendra, Krishna, *vīṇā*; Charlie Mariano, saxophone; Jamey Haddad and Glen Velez, percussion. www.raghasmusic.com.
Rajamani, Oliver, songwriter. *Pakiam.* www.oliverrajamani.com.
Ramaswamy, Prasanna, electric guitar. www.guitarprasanna.com.

Ravikiran, N., chitravina; Jovino Santos Neto, piano; Glen Velez, G. Harishankar, and Poovalur Srinivasan, percussion. *Rays and Forays*. Naxos World. www.naxos.com.

Subramaniam, L., violin; Larry Coryell, guitar. *From the Ashes*. Water Lily Acoustics.

———. *Live in Moscow*. Pan Music (includes *Fantasy on Vedic Chants*).

CD-ROM, VCD

Kersenboom, Saskia, producer. *Devadasi Murai: Remembering Devadasis*. CD-ROM. Indira Gandhi National Centre for the Arts, Delhi. www.ignca.nic.in

Saint Tyagaraja—A Multimedia Presentation. CD-ROM. Contact Dr. Shivkumar Kalyanaraman, 980 Birchwood Lane, Niskayuna, NY 12309; http://tyagarajaproject.weblogs.com or haravu@newgenlib.com.

Shashikiran, N., and S. Sowmya, producers. *Nadanubhava*, CD-ROM; and *Nadopasana*, VCD. www.carnatica.com/arcade-main.htm.

Viewing

Altar of Fire (film on Vedic fire sacrifice). Mystic Fire Video. www.mysticfire.com.

Balasaraswati (Bharata Nāṭyam Dance). World Music Archives, Wesleyan University, Middletown, CT 06459; telephone: 860-685-3826.

Catlin, Amy, and Fredric Lieberman, producers. *South Indian Classical Music: House Concert with M. D. Ramanathan*. Apsara Media for Intercultural Education, 13659 Victory Boulevard, Suite #577, Van Nuys, CA 91401; fax: 818-785-1495.

———. *T. N. Krishnan, Violinist. At Home with Master Musicians of Madras, Volume 1*. Apsara Media for Intercultural Education.

Catlin, Amy, and Nazir Jairazbhoy, producers. *The Bake Restudy: 1938–1984: The Preservation and Transformation of Tradition in Tamilnadu, Kerala, and Karnataka*. Apsara Media for Intercultural Education.

JVC Video Anthology of Music and Dance (South Asia, volumes 11, 12, 13). Distributed by Rounder Records.

Kasthuri: A South Indian Film Star. Association for Asian Studies, 1995.

Kathakali: South Indian Dance-Drama from the Kerala Kalamandalam. Asia Society, New York.

Nelson, David. *Mrdangam Mind: The Tani Avartanam in Karnatak Music*. Contact the author c/o Music Department, Wesleyan University, Middletown, CT 06459.

Rhythms Divine: Temple Arts of Kerala. Five videocassette set of Kēraḷa percussion ensembles. www.rhythmsdivine.com: telephone 765-452-4026.

Rukmini Kalyanan: Ballet Dance Drama, by the Kuchipudi Art Academy, Chennai. Sri Venkateswara Temple, Pittsburgh, PA.

Viswanathan, T. *Discovering the Music of India.* Directed by Bernard Wilets, 1969. www.buyindies.com/listings/8/7/AIMS-8705.html.

Zarrilli, Phillip B. *An Introduction to Kathakali Dance Drama.* www.routledge.com.

———. *Killing of Kirmira.* www.routledge.com.

Films Available from the Center for South Asia, University of Wisconsin (www.wisc.edu/southasia/films/index.html)

Bearing the Heat: Mother Goddess Worship in South India

Lady of Gingee: South Indian Draupadi Festivals

Modern Brides: Arranged Marriage in South India

Pilgrimage to Pittsburgh (on the anniversary of the founding of the Sri Venkatesvara temple)

Wedding of the Goddess (reenactment of Minakshi's wedding to Śiva in the city of Madurai)

Other

Internet Purchase of Audio CDs and Films on DVD/VCD

www.ayngaran.com

www.indiaplaza.com

www.indofilms.com

www.nehaflix.com

www.vistaindia.com (affiliated with Raaga Music Megastores in New York, New Jersey, and California.

Internet Links to Educational, Cultural, and Research Organizations

www.aradhana.org, Cleveland Tyagaraja Aradhana (Ohio)

www.archive-india.org/arce_resources.html, Archives and Research Centre for Ethnomusicology, American Institute of Indian Studies (Delhi)

www.brhad.org, Brhaddhvani, Research and Training Centre of Music of the World (Chennai)

www.ignca.nic.in, Indira Gandhi National Centre for the Arts (Delhi)

www.kalamandalam.com, The Kerala Kalamandalam, Center for Indian Performing Arts and Culture (Cheruthuruthy, Kēraḷa)

www.musicacademymadras.org, The Madras Music Academy (Chennai)

www.sampradaya.org, Sampradaya Centre for South Indian music traditions (Chennai)

www.sruti.com, Sruti magazine of Indian music and dance (Chennai)

www.tfmpage.com/home.html, Tamiḻ film music page

Websites on Karṇāṭak Music, Maintained by Karṇāṭak Musicians

www.carnatic.com

www.carnatica.com

www.carnaticcorner.com
www.euronet.nl/users/l_pesch
www.medieval.org/music/world/carnatic.html
www.narada.org
www.sangeetham.com

Author's Website (Additional Listening Guides and Activities)
www.wheatoncollege.edu/Faculty/MatthewAllen.html

Index

Italic page numbers denote illustrations.